JUST FOR U

Joe Barnes

Super PRO-crastinators

An Almost Complete Guide

To NOT Getting Things Done- On Time

By

Joseph E. Barnes

First Edition

January 1985

Published by:

BARNES BOOKS

Fort Ann, N.Y. 12827

Library of Congress Catalog Card Number 84-71554

ISBN: 0-917732-34-0 Casebound

ISBN: 0-917732-35-9 Paperback

Copyright 1984 by J. E. Barnes
Printed in the United States of America

READ WHAT OTHERS HAVE TO SAY ABOUT THIS BOOK

The reason you are reading nothing is:

1. I'm waiting to hear from YOU.

2. Coneco Laser Graphics printed this entire book so fast, it made no sense to send traditional 'galley proofs' to professional reviewers.

3. Same as YOU, they can review from this fully completed first edition.

4. This new high-tech electronic printing process will revolutionize the book manufacturing industry.

5. It gives YOU a chance to be quoted and (maybe) have your name in the second edition.

ABOUT THIS BOOK

I could have — and should have written this book a long time ago. I contemplated doing it at an early age. But I put it off and put it off; and dilly dallied as long as I could — much in the tradition of my ancestors.

My ancestors had contemplated writing this book thru three-and-a-half millenia of footdragging.

I will not give you all their names as is done in Genesis. But I can tell you that Lord Barnaby Barnes, Lord Mayor of London in 1712, came very close to having it published. Apparently, he just kept waiting for a more favorable time.

In the meantime, it was Lord Barnaby who first established the great SuperPRO-crastinators HALLOWED HALL OF HESITATION.

This page of this book is
dedicated in his memory.

Before that time, Joseph E. Boujourne, who invaded England in the year 1066 with William the Conqueror, tried writing it — but delayed doing so until he could learn to speak English and spell his name properly.

Thus you see, my heritage endowed me with the obligation to write it.

For years, others were able to postpone this obligation with the excuse, 'Ancestors have accumulated too much data on the subject of procrastination. How in the world can I sort it all out?'

'That's easy,' replied one member of our clan. 'Buy a word processing computer.'

He even provided me with a book called, 'The Word Processing Book'. It is so well written, even I can understand it. It convinced me.

Yet, it seemed appropriate to postpone purchase until a more favorable time. It would be sacrilege to erase the considered delays of centuries through the magic of modern technology — in one brief orgy.

So I put it off until I could organize a team to research current practices among today's procrastinators — many of whom you may know.

Mainly through unobtrusive observation (snooping politely) I was able to supplement the data gathering of my research team.

It soon became apparent that there was great need for an epistle dealing with the subject. Nearly everyone was into some phase of procrastination. Yet only two books could be found on the subject.

I decided it would be counter productive to write a ponderous tome. So I decided to write a well illustrated guidebook called 'How to Procrastinate More Effectively'. Thus it would be compatible with my previous seventeen books.

After a bit more stalling, I bought a Word Processing Computer. It was mind boggling for me to discover what can be accomplished with a Word Processor.

Lightning fast checking and correction of spelling; No retyping of messy pages; Instant moving of entire blocks of text to more suitable locations; Instant everything.

Well, not everything. A writer still must go through the torture of thinking.

Torture be damned. This book had to be written — if for no other reason — to let lonely closet procrastinators know that they should not hide in shame.

Why make wretched souls of those who practice procrastination? Is it not better that they should look in a mirror and laugh at themselves?

Perhaps the very act of dealing lightly with this worldwide phenomenon will improve the self-image of those who have been brain washed into believing 'nothing good ever comes of delay'.

If you are doing a poor job of procrastinating, you will learn how to improve your techniques by emulating characters in this book.

The scenarios on these pages discourage allegiance to doom and gloom. Better that we face life as it is — and deal with it from a position of strength, joy and happiness.

My ancestors want you to know that they would have given you the same message — had they been granted more time.

They are justifiably envious of the tremendous time-saver now at my disposal. And they rest in peace knowing that the Word Processing Computer makes it possible for me to complete a book in far less than a year. In fact, two books.

To honor Lord Barnaby, and revive his HALLOWED HALL OF HESITATION for SuperPROS, a national club had to be organized, and SuperPRO recognition granted.

Paradoxically, some members have already taken on a whole new life. Now, they hardly ever procrastinate.

Can this book also cure YOU and your friends of procrastination? Maybe! A lot depends on you. The book is loaded with subliminal messages.

In any event, you can have a lot of fun reading about someone you may know.

I did.

HEADQUARTERS

The Headquarters for Super PRO Crastinators Club of North America is appropriately located in a log cabin complex nestled in the foothills of the Adirondack Mountains of upstate New York.

Here on a woodland estate within the six million acre Adirondack State Park, the author finds peace and tranquility in great abundance — idyllic for a writer.

ACKNOWLEDGEMENTS

Many people helped to make this book possible. Most important of all is my wife, Grace, whose tolerance and understanding, has made it possible for me to procrastinate endlessly about other things so as to devote ceaseless effort to my writing.

Had it not been for the urging of John Barnes, and Len Ramsey, I would not have obtained a Word Processor to make the task so much easier. Brian Clements, Dick Guay, and Ellen Nichols, of Foothills Computers were infinitely patient in teaching me how to use the equipment.

My researchers prefer anonymity, but I can at least reveal that Carol, Mike, June, Penny, Richard, and Susie all provided me with important research material. Kathy was most helpful on the college scene.

George Beyerbach and Max Tupper gave technical assistance, which may have seemed minor to them, but was important to me.

Books written by William L. Zinsser, and Peter A. McWilliams inspired me more than they will ever know.

Penny and Joel were picky and demanding (especially Joel) in proof-reading and editing of final copy.

And I wish I could find a way to tell my Dad how much his inspiration, guidance, and encouragement have meant to me.

I appreciate the combined efforts of all these people, even though they prevented me from postponing publication — until some distant tomorrow.

CONTENTS

SuperPROS AT HOME

CONTENTS

SuperPROS AT COLLEGE

SuperPROS AT WORK

CONTENTS

SuperPROS EVERYWHERE

SuperPRO

Well, you've finally got around to reading this book.

The fact that you've been meaning to do so for quite some time is a good sign. You may have the makings of a truly bonafide procrastinator. Even if you have not developed the technique sufficiently to become recognized as a SuperPRO, don't despair. There is hope if you keep practicing.

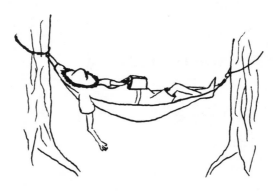

A SuperPRO is someone who has mastered the art of NOT GETTING THINGS DONE — ON TIME someone who always puts things off until tomorrow — the next day — next week — or even later; and has a record to prove it.

There are some who are natural born champions in the gentle art of procrastinating. They will be hard to compete against. However, this guidebook (unlike any other I know) will give you a chance to compete eye-ball-to-eye-ball with the best of them. Not only compete, but also BECOME RECOGNIZED for your achievements.

What other book does that?

If you know of any, I'd appreciate hearing from you —
if you ever get around to dropping me a note. No hurry.

 FIRST: Of course, before you can compete, you must become eligible. The first eligibility requirement is shown on the next page.

 SECOND: A second requirement is that you read this book from cover to cover — whenever you get around to it.

 THIRD· The third is that you be able to produce two reliable witnesses who will certify that you have an unblemished record of NOT doing things — on time.

Then you must earn the right to become listed among
the 10 BEST PROCRASTINATORS OF THE WEEK.

If your ultimate goal is to have your picture and name
placed in the SuperPRO-crastinators HALLOWED HALL
OF HESITATION, (which is equal to the SuperPro Hall of
Fame), you will learn how it can be done.

Yes, I am going to show you how you can become qualified. But right now, I'll put that off 'til later.

Why? Because I am a SuperPRO myself. You don't
want me to wreck my image do you? Besides, I want you
to get on with reading the rest of this book. You need to
develop a background of knowledge and a sense of belong-
ing before you enter into such serious competition.

Your instructions will be buried somewhere in the text
— whenever I get around to doing it.

In the meantime, we will deal with the subject on a
RAM basis. That's computerese. And if you don't know
what it means, it's time you did. After all we are living in
an age of computerization and it's high time you learned
at least a little of the basic language. So go look up RAM.

While you are doing that I can goof off from my typing
for at least a little while.

LEO

ARIES

SCORPIO

WHO
CAN BECOME
A
SuperPRO?

Several million
people
procrastinate
almost daily
BUT
only those who
are born under
Zodiac signs
shown here
are eligible
ALL OTHERS
procrastinate
at your own
risk. Sorry!

SAGITTARIUS

PISCES

TAURUS

GEMINI

VIRGO

LIBRA

CAPRICORN

CANCER

AQUARIUS

14

Did you look up RAM — yet?

Probably not!

See, you already qualify yourself as a neophyte procrastinator. So I guess I better let you know what RAM means. I don't want you to feel guilty about not having looked it up.

RAM means Random Access Memory.

So taking a very broad and liberal interpretation of RAM, I am going to access my memory and my research files dealing with procrastination — on a random basis.

That's how you and I are going to deal with this subject of procrastination. Strictly on a random basis. There will be no pragmatic, tightly structured text insisting that your mind follow a flow of words in lockstep dogma. We who are schooled in the delights of procrastination want to enjoy the freedom of individuality in developing our own field of expertise within this discipline.

So let's get with it.

WHO PROCRASTINATES?

From your own observations, you have probably noted that many, many people have developed at least a minor degree of proficiency in the art of procrastination.

To name only a few, this will include most of your friends, relatives, classmates, acquaintances, business associates, bosses, politicians, lawyers, garage mechanics, — — — and sometimes even your lovers.

Where have all these people acquired this skill?

Certainly it is not being taught in the classroom. At least not officially.

LIKE SEX

Do you suppose it is like sex? A lot of people practice sex without any formalized instructions. Not that instructors with illustrated lessons would be hard to come by.

True it is that schools do now devote a fair degree of time to sex education. And that is good. But a true appreciation of (and may I say) 'the joy of sex' can not be fully appreciated from classroom text or lectures. Sex is something that has to be experienced in order to fully appreciate it.

That's how it is with procrastination. You can't just read about it, or think about it. In order to get the real flavor of it you have to plunge right in.

No sense in being weak-hearted about it. You might better recognize, right up front, that procrastinators are skillful time wasters.

IS TIME MONEY?

If you want to become a skillful world class SuperPROcr-astinator, you need to develop a nearly total disregard for TIME. Pay no heed to those who say, 'Time is money.'.

You can even overlook the fact that several banks in your area constantly bombard you with advertisements offering to pay you interest for Time Deposits.

Well, they won't!

If you want to prove this to yourself and at the same time give your friendly neighborhood banker apoplexy, just walk into the bank lobby pushing a wheelbarrow.

In answer to the banker's less-than friendly stare and perplexed curiosity, simply say, 'I've got a wheelbarrow full of Time. Where do I deposit it?'.

'But . . . but . . . but . . . you misunderstood,' or some less noble phrase will be the banker's reply.

Now I ask you, 'Where's the truth in advertising?' If a bank advertises something you certainly have a right to expect them to know how to handle it. Don't you?

After all, if it is true that 'Time is Money', wouldn't it be wise for a banker to let any frugal procrastinator save time rather than waste it?

Sure it would.

Then, when the procrastinator gets around to needing some time (probably desperately), he could make a fast withdrawal and put it to use when he needs it most.

Ben Franklin

SuperPROS AT HOME

I suspect some of you would prefer to get your training in procrastination on a step-by-step basis, as is done in several of my 'How-To' books.

Unfortunately, procrastination does not lend itself to that technique. It is something very unique, and can only thoroughly be portrayed through the mirror of life.

I like that. It's a lot more fun getting in on the action. It may become confusing at times. But so does life.

So let's place our mirror in a typical American home and concentrate our attention on an arena guaranteed to be familiar to virtually every individual from sea to shining sea.

THE GREAT DISH DODGE

Let's start with what is known as the Great Dish Dodge. Most of us at one time or another have been willing participants in this charade.

It is so prevalent throughout the land that Congress has considered the possibility of recognizing it as a National Pastime. Passage of a referendum is almost assured once women of our great republic have gained equal representation in the House of Representatives.

Uncle Ralph was the first to bring it to my attention.

Although not a participant in the Great Dish Dodge, Uncle Ralph can still be rated an expert on the subject.

How come?

Because for forty-one years of his married life, he was a keen observer of all the magnificent ploys that surround this most exclusive field of procrastination. He considered it exclusively the province of womenfolk. Therefore he was exempt from any involvement or opportunity to add points to his already significant collection of well earned credits for procrastination.

Uncle Ralph never did dishes.

That was 'woman's work' And no matter how much he envied them for the thrice daily opportunity to gain SuperPRO points, he never made the slightest attempt to set sail upon such holy water.

He is that kind of man. He respects the rights of others.

Uncle Ralph clearly illustrated that when he first pointed out the Great Dish Dodge to me.

He said, 'Young man, I've noticed that every time Aunt Mildred invites you over here for Sunday dinner, you jump right up from the table and offer to help her with the dinner dishes.'

'Yeah. Well I just want to show her how much I appreciate her wonderful cooking.'

'No need to over do it! You've already shown her that every time you take a third helping.'

'Yeah, but Uncle Ralph, doing the dishes ain't that big a deal.'

'It is to Aunt Mildred. It's one of her responsibilities. I know she'll never even complain. But what you're doing is forcing her to do the dishes before she's really ready.'

'That can't be. I'm making the job twice as easy for her.'

'Maybe so. And maybe not.' replied Uncle Ralph. 'Ya see, she rather relishes putting off doing the dishes until she gets darned good and ready. Gives her something to sort of look forward to after a big meal.'

'I know Aunt Mildred loves to cook. But doing the dishes is something else,' I said.

Uncle Ralph leaned back in his lounger, took a couple of puffs on his pipe and said, 'Could be. Nevertheless they just naturally go together.'

'Well sorta,' I agreed.

He continued. 'You see son, folks have just gotta look forward to things they know they're gonna have to do sooner or later.'

'That's true.'

'It's just as important to be able to postpone things 'til you are in the mood to do 'em.'

'But isn't that procrastination?''Sure is! Does a body a lotta good though.'

'How's that?'

'Take Aunt Mildred and her dishes. Last Sunday's dinner was great. Her cookin' is always great. But she wan't forced to jump right up from the meal and do dishes. Do you know what she did?'

'No. What?'

'She left the dishes right on the table went outside and puttered around in her flower beds. An hour later she came in and stacked 'em on the counter next to the sink.'

'The food must have been stuck on pretty good by then.'

'Probably.'

'Did she rinse them before she stacked them?'

'Nope. She was tryin' to find a way to get out of doin' 'em. Both girls had run off to Sunday afternoon practice on some play they're goin' to be in at school.

'So she was faced with a bit of a challenge. You always are when you try to get outa doing somethin' you're supposed to do. Kinda helps to keep life interestin .

'So instead of doin' anythin' more about the dishes, your Aunt Mildred just let 'em set while she concentrated on somethin' she's a knittin'.

'What's she knitting?'

20

'Don't know. Don't matter. Point is she always finds somethin' else important to do while she's tryin' to get outa doin' anythin' she don't wanta do.'

'Wouldn't it just be easier to do the dishes right away?' I asked.

'Sure. But then she ends up in a rut. Nothing but a routine task. No imaginative delayin' tactics to challenge her sense of accomplishment.'

'So what did Aunt Mildred do?'

'She waited another coupla hours while I was watchin' the ball game. Then she went over and made a lot of noise rinsin' and stackin' the dishes. Didn't bother me none. Game wan't so good anyway.

'Just gave her a chance to grumble and get some bitchiness outa her system.'

'Everybody needs to do that once in a while.'

'Then she did the dishes. Right?'

'No. No.', replied Uncle Ralph. 'Your Aunt Mildred is smarter'n that. She just waited 'til the girls got home from school.

'June, she's the clever one, said she'd be glad to help except she had so much homework that needed to be done. Too bad she had used that same excuse the night before, cause it didn't work this time.'

I wonder if teachers realize what an enormous amount of homework — distasteful as it may be — is done by young ladies bent on doing most anything to dodge doing dishes.

Uncle Ralph added, 'You know, after the three of them got through hemming and hawing and making excuses, they settled down to doing those dishes. Then they started singing and laughing long past when the last dish was washed, dried and put away.'

'Did you join in?'

'Nah. They got such great voices, I just like to listen and watch my womenfolk enjoying themselves.'

My research team reports that this scene (and many variations of it) takes place in millions of homes everyday. No wonder Congress is trying to gain proper recognition for this important contribution to procrastination.

There are a lot of votes out there. Daily practitioners are sure to remember those who voted for recognition.

If you are not yet into the Dish Dodge, take a crack at it. The opportunity for daily practice is everywhere. Don't overlook it if you are going for SuperPRO.

WHEN IT'S TIME TO DO DISHES, HERE ARE A FEW THINGS YOU CAN DO TO QUALIFY AS A COMPETENT DISH DODGER:

Go to the bathroom — don't rush it.
Sponge off the stove top.
Inspect your finger nails.
Brush the crumbs off the table.
Check the refrigerator — for anything.
Change the paper towels.
Put on more comfortable shoes.
Refill the paper napkin holder.
Water the plants — in the kitchen, in the dining room, the living room, the bath room, — anywhere you can find them.
use a small watering can for the above, and be sure to make several trips.
Dust the dining room furniture.
Check the wall calendar for next week's appointments.
Phone your sister.
Unplug the toaster.
Make a pot of coffee.
Try talking to your husband.
Talk to yourself — if necessary.

See how easy it is to become immersed in the Great Dish Dodge by simply applying your talents to other worthy pursuits.

In our day and age, when discrimination is not permitted, the above activities and other acceptable maneuvers, are no longer the sole property of the fairer sex.

Any man who wishes to embrace them is at full liberty to do so. Anytime. Anywhere.

THE TIDY HOUSE

Now that we have found our way into the American home, let's take a look at a little more of our controlled research.

A young couple — much much younger than Uncle Ralph and Aunt Mildred — have given us permission to use our hidden camera. That is if we do not use their names.

So in compliance with that request they will be referred to only by their initials.

Richard O.C. is probably the more accomplished procrastinator, both because he is a bit older than his wife, Lynn D.C., and has been to college. He was an outstanding athlete. Made All American in his freshman and sophomore years.

Injury, however, removed him from the starting lineup in his junior year. His knee gave him so much trouble that it was almost impossible for him to scurry his 275 pound, six foot six frame back to the huddle.

Why is it that every coach insists that everybody be in the huddle? After all, Richard knew all the plays. A quick whisper would have set him straight.

Lack of violent exercise provided him with a surplus of energy to apply to his studies. But he seldom got around to it. He is still meaning to go back to finish up his degree.

Lynn D.C. was a brilliant high school student. Had to transfer to a much bigger school for her senior year because by the middle of her junior year she had used up all the courses her central high had to offer.

She took top honors as a brilliant transfer student without ever cracking a homework book. She then decided college would not be much of a challenge and went to work instead.

Be that as it may, Richard O.C. and Lynn D.C. are a very happy couple. Both are very happy in what they do.

He is a quality control engineer; very good at it and highly respected throughout the industry.

He never permits any correction of a problem to be postponed. If a re-run or a revision of any kind is necessary, he insists that it be done immediately. He is nice about it. Why not? Maybe his mere size helps get the message across anyway.

Top management is looking at him with loving eyes. His future is assured.

Lynn has likewise been identified for upward mobility in one of the top 500 firms in the nation. Her keen-eyed boss rates her as 'superior in every respect — the most thoroughly organized individual I have everseen in all my years with Crown.'

'Nothing is ever left undone. She always completes her work on time and is generally ahead of schedule.'

How do these two exemplary young people rate mention among the procrastinators of the world?

It's true that they will garner nothing but demerits if they attempt to compete in any way for an annual award in any segment of the Business Division of Procrastinators Club of North America.

But within the sanctum sanctorum of their own home,they have already established themselves as worthy contestants for a top award.

If you pay an unannounced visit to their home, you can judge for yourself.

Here is what you will see:

LYING ON THE LIVING ROOM FLOOR

Three size fourteen sneakers.
Two size fourteen hiking boots.
Three pair of high heeled shoes.
One pair of ladies sandals.
One large wool sock.
Sports section of Sunday's N.Y. Times. (It is now
      Thursday evening.)
Two hand-carved hiking sticks.
Last month's House Beautiful Magazine.
One opened -to-dry red umbrella. (It rained a week
      ago.)
A hammer and two screw drivers.
One almost empty bowl of popcorn.
A sleeping tiger cat.
A puppy chewing on a fourth sneaker.
A book on Acid Rain.
Probably a rug underneath it all.

ON THE DINING ROOM TABLE

Four seed catalogs.
Three wood carving knives.
A partially balanced check book.
Three stacks of checks.
An unfinished cross-word puzzle.
Three empty beer cans.
Two empty coke bottles.
A bright red Azalea plant. A beauty.
One pair of vice grips.
An empty shopping bag. Sears.

A disassembled flashlight. Batteries
A quilting pattern.
A road map. Spread out.
Five overdue library books.
Several unopened pieces of mail.
Tickets to Saturday night's hockey game.

IN THE KITCHEN

Dirty dishes.
Lots of dirty dishes. (Piled high in both sink wells.)
Unwashed pots and pans. (On either side of the sink.)
More dishes. (Undried and out of sight in the dish-
        washer beneath the sink.)
Two kettles on the stove top. (Might be clean.)
Bottles stacked on either side of the
nearly hidden electric stove. (To be returned for de-
        posit.)
An uncovered half-eaten cake. (No flies.)
Two partially rinsed tomato soup cans.
Three sharp knives on a cutting board.
Four slices of bread near a toaster.
Two dying plants. Unwatered.
Countertop space — none visible.
Quarantine — highly recommended.

BEAUTIFUL BATHROOM

Toilet seat up. (Very inconsiderate.)
Vanity mirror clean — spotless.
Shaving mirror streaked with spots of toothpaste.
Hairdyer on vanity table top.
Curlers everywhere — on vanity, on window sill, on
        toilet tank top, four on the floor.
Gooey soap bar on sink edge.
Drippy wash cloth above electric heater.

Two wet bath towels. (Flung over shower rod.)
Wadded-up bath mat.
No toilet paper. (Whadaya mean — no toilet paper?)
Sorry! Very sorry! NO TOILET PAPER!

No matter how high you rise in the ranks of SuperPROS, never,never postpone putting in an adequate supply of toilet tissue. Whether it be at home, the office, the mill, the safari, or anywhere else, if you neglect this responsibility, you are sure to do down to defeat.

Previously classified papers now reveal that Napoleon's shameful defeat at the battle of Waterloo may have been caused by a foot-dragging supply officer who failed to get his T-Paper Requisiton Form 7/436A-22P filed on time. The result. No Toilet Paper.

So on the morning of June 18, 1815 the greatest military genius of his time had nothing behind him but an army of dispirited disenchanted, 'tissueless' soldiers.

How could they be expected to fight under these conditions?

Nevertheless, the domineering little Nappy pushed them into combat. They fought. But they had lost the will to win. Before sunset, Napoleon's last great campaign ground to a bloody and dirty end.

They lost. And you know the rest of the story.

If you are to become a SuperPRO, take a lesson from history and do your foot-dragging elsewhere.

Let's get back to the present. Would you like to take a peek into Richard's Den?

Mind you, just a peek now. DON'T ENTER!

RICHARD'S DEN

An enormous mahogany desk. A beauty.

Posters. Giant posters. Little posters. Colored posters.
(None X-rated.)

Three fine briar pipes.

A large can of Sir Walter tobacco. (Richard has not
smoked for over three years.)

A pile of Sports Illustrated.

More magazines — Organic Gardening, Yankee,
Baron's, Changing Times.

300 pounds of weights in the middle of the floor. (Real
ankle busters in the dark for anyone who dared
enter this inner sanctum.)

A typewriter with what appears to be a half written
letter.

A memo pad THINGS TO DO TODAY — 12 items
(Dated 10 days ago — four items crossed off.)

A camera. Telephoto lens and all.

Several 8 x 10 photos scattered across the desk. Some
negatives also.

A scattering of pocket change.

Four one dollar bills.

Leaning against one wall — a mammoth bulletin
board packed with buttons —

All kinds — political, advertising, clever, cute, funny,
ridiculous, etc . . .

In the corner —

A baseball bat.
A catcher's mitt.
A tennis racquet.
A football.
A basketball.
Six tennis balls.
A fishing rod & reel.
A bowling ball.
Maybe more.

THEIR BEDROOM

A king size bed. Unmade.
Heirloom quilt. Mostly on the floor.
His and her bathrobes. Tossed carelessly across the
    bed.
Two dressers. Four drawers open with garments pro-
    truding.
A black negligee draped over the headboard. (Appar-
    ently worn no more than ten or twelve min-
    utes.)
Two closets with folding doors. Open.
HERS jammed tight with many colorful garments.
    Some obviously expensive.
HIS — very orderly except for several neckties thrown
    over the clothes rod, along with a pair of pants
    and some kind of oddball shirt. Also at one end
    of his closet — several very feminine dresses.
    Strange.
The floor is something else. Strewn with two very
    large slippers, several pair of ladies shoes, a
    half-slip, a man's shirt (three buttons missing)
    and other assorted pieces of clothing both large
    and small.

Incredible!

It is almost impossible to thread one's way to any location in the room without tripping over some article of clothing on the floor.

A tornado watcher would rate this well above an amateur status.

Have you ever made a surprise visit to anyone's house and seen such a shambles?

Does it remind you of anyone you know?

(If so, please send me their name and address. I have a little gift for them.)

No need to take you into other areas of the house such as the guest room, the laundry, the basement, or the sewing room. You get the picture. Don't you?

Richard O. C. and Lynn D. C. have several guests coming Saturday evening.

You may wonder why such capable and talented people have been so dilatory in their own home. Especially when they have gained such an enviable reputation for prompt performance in the work place.

Can it be that 'enough is enough'? They just needed to set aside an area of their lives where they would not have to operate constantly 'with a sense of urgency'.

Controlled procrastination provides an exceptionally good method for escaping the pressure pot of the business world. Or so I am told.

Business moguls will disagreee with this. Some of them work like hell at everything. They make a lot of money. Many die young. For what?

R.O.C. and Lynn have provided themselves with a safety valve. It also gives them a chance to compete in at least one category for Procrastinators of the Year.

Psychiatrists, psychologists, psychotherapists and the like will likewise disagree with the theory of potential goodness from controlled procrastinating. One of their missions in life seems to be to overcome procrastination — at least on the part of their clients.

Yet an eminent member of that profession says, 'THERE SEEMS TO BE NO UNIVERSALLY EFFECTIVE METHOD TO OVERCOME PROCRASTINATION.'

If that is so, isn't it much better to take a positive approach to the phenomenon and put it to work for ourselves?

I would hope so. There certainly is one heck of a lot of people who seem to be willing to take it under advisement.

GOOD INTENTIONS

In a court of law, you could be asked, 'What is your intent?'

And that is indeed a very important first question. It strikes at the very heart of legitimate procrastination.

Whatever you are currently postponing must be something you truly intend to do — at some future time.

You can say any of the following:

tomorrow
later
real soon

sometime later on
after I finish this
when the time is ripe
when I feel in the mood
as soon as I can get around to it

Whatever you do, do not commit yourself to a specific date. It will leave you no room for maneuvering. Furthermore, if you expect to obtain and retain membership in SuperPROS of America, don't get off on the wrong foot by violating rule number five, which states, 'AVOID COMMITTING YOURSELF TO A TIME OR PLACE FOR THE COMPLETION OF A POSTPONED ACTION'.

The most important thing to remember is that you do truly intend to complete the action. No matter what it is.

If all you are doing is making excuses to avoid doing something that you have no intention whatsoever of doing, then you are not worthy of consideration for fraternizing with procrastinators at any level.

You may be nothing more than a compulsive liar.

Or worse yet. Just damned lazy.

Be that as it may. Remember, and remember it well. GOOD INTENTIONS are the foundation stones on which this everlasting edifice is built. Pay them faithful homage.

HOUSEHOLD CHORES

Charlie Green brought up the subject of being busy around the house, let's drop in on him and get a bird's eye view of what does happen at his house.

What we see may even bring to mind some other household you know.

Charlie has a beautiful wife. She is a real knockout — and a lot younger than he is. Her name is Gertrude. She is only four years older than his daughter and is often mistaken as her sister. Surprisingly, this pleases both of them.

They call his wife, 'Gee-Gee' — not because of her initials, but because of her former profession.

You would expect that she would be the last to drag her tail out of bed in the morning. Not so.

Promptly at 5:30, she jumps out of bed; slips into a bright pink sweat suit; dashes out the kitchen door; opens the iron gate; gives a whistle; and runs merrily down the country blacktop road.

What an inviting target for an amorous mugger — or an early morning pickup driver on his way to work.

They gawk. And they yearn. Some may even plan. But somehow they feel it's wise to put it off until another time.

They see an object several yards ahead of her and a second one gliding gracefully a few yards behind her.

What is there about those two sleek black Doberman Pinchers that seems to so unduly influence their decisions?

Too bad. Those eager dogs love fresh meat.

Back at the house after her two mile run, Gee-Gee strips off the sweat suit; lets it fall to the bathroom floor; and takes a stinging hot and cold shower.

Two quick eggs, sunnyside up, two dark brown toast, and a cup of black coffee are next. No orange juice this morning. She left it sitting on the counter yesterday — and it is still there.

'Doesn't anybody around here ever pick up anything?' she asks herself.

She hears the shower running and knows that Susan is up. But not a sound from her kid brother Tommy's room — so Gee Gee taps on his door and says, 'Better get it in gear young man, or you'll be late for school.'

'Who cares?' he answers.

'I do! Now move it!'

His feet hit the floor loud and clear. It's great to have someone like Gee Gee 'care'.

When she arrives at the office, someone asks her, 'How can you ever eat such a huge breakfast?'

'Easy. Exercise. Keeps you in shape. And if you are going to eat big, do it in the morning. You'll burn it off during the day,' she answers.

And as a bonus, men in the office often dig in to help her find any missing items.

It would be nice if the same were true at home.

When she arrives, it's raining and she can't even put the car in the garage. One of Charlie's 'wood projects' is still blocking the entrance.

Dripping wet, she storms into the house and says, 'Charlie, you promised me you would have that garage cleaned up today.'

'I planned to, Honey, but when we heard it was going to rain, we had to get our golf game in early. Just got home a few minutes ago myself. I'll do it tomorrow.'

'That's what you've been saying for two weeks.'

'I know. But this time I mean it.'

'Sure you do. How about doing it this evening?'

'Good idea, Honey. I'll do it right after I take my nap. I had a hard day on the course today.'

She went into the bathroom intending to get out of her wet clothes. 'Ye Gods.' She said, 'Doesn't anybody around here ever pick up anything? My sweat suit's still on the floor by the shower.'

She got into something more comfortable and went into the kitchen hoping that maybe Susan had started supper. 'What's that awful smell?', she asked.

'Must be the garbage from last night,' replied Charlie.

'Didn't the plumber come to fix the disposal?'

'Not yet.'

'Did you call him?'

'I was going to, but I wasn't sure what time I would get home from golf, so I think it's better to wait until tomorrow.'

'But you've already been waiting five days. Tell me truly now. Just WHEN are you going to get the plumber over here?'

'Hun, why press me?' said Charlie, 'You know I got good intentions. Things just get delayed sometimes. You know how it is.'

'I sure do. But on this, I need a firm answer.'

'Okay. Tomorrow — for sure.'

'That's a little better than SOMETIME SOON — but not much.

Teenager Tommy bopped into the room at that moment and said, 'Jeez, things around here are a mess. Why don't we get this place picked up — you know, organized?

Susan arrived on the scene as Tommy was talking and asked, 'What turned you on, squirt? Should we start with your room?'

'Okay by me,' he replied. 'I been planning on doing it anyway.'

'Planning — you've been promising ever since you were ten.'

'Yeah. I was just a kid then. It's okay to put off doing things when you're a kid, but now as adults, we should develop a sense of responsibility, and never let things get in such a mess.'

'Listen to HIM.' said Susan.

'You're right, Susan,' said Gee Gee. 'Let's listen to him. Even better, let's have Tommy make a list of all the things he sees that need to be done around here.'

Tommy made his list.

But he went one step beyond — maybe two steps beyond what was expected of him. He tagged the undone deeds with the name of the guilty party. Tied to this was a plan of action for the future.

He said, 'I'm not going to post this list. Instead, I propose we discuss the list and each of us volunteer to do certain chores around the house.'

Charlie was amazed — and proud.

He said to himself, 'I wonder if this fifteen year old kid realizes he's involved himself in management? He's getting things DONE — through other people. That's what management is all about.'

So with pride, he leaned forward to listen to Tommy's proposals.

Tommy said, 'Right now, the worst area is the garage. But let's leave that 'til later and deal with our living quarters.'

'Which part?' asked Susan fearing it might be a subtle attack on her room.

'The kitchen,' he replied. 'First comes the garbage disposal — Dad?'

'Okay. I'll get the plumber tomorrow for sure.'

'There's a drawer handle missing. Would it take long to fix it, Dad?'

'Not too long. I got it downstairs on my bench. I could probably do that tomorrow also.'

'Now comes the matter of dirty dishes,' continued Tommy. 'We always seem to have a lot of them.'

'Well,' said Susan, 'We could take turns. I could do them on Mondays and Tuesdays.'

'Okay,' said Tommy. 'I'll take the next two days.'

Smart kids, thought Gee Gee. That means I get the big weekend duty. Charlie will never volunteer for this.

And he didn't.

Then without any prompting, Susan said, 'I'll see to setting the table every day, unless I'm late getting home from a school activity.'

'The waste basket is always full and overflowing,' said Tommy. 'It will be my chore to empty it often.'

'No one ever puts the bread back in the bread box — or the cookies — or the crackers or the cereal — or any of that stuff away. I'll do that,' said Susan.

'Anybody — ANYBODY who has a snack after supper cleans up after themselves — that means, dishes, bottles, boxes, papers — everything. Okay Dad?'

'Sure.'

Charlie thought, 'My God what's got into these kids? What do they want?'

To Gee Gee, it was too good to be true. 'Will they do it?' she wondered.

'The bathroom is next,' said Tommy. 'No more gooey bars of soap. No more wet towels over the shower curtain. No more clothes, or shoes, or slippers on the floor. No one uses the sink without cleaning it off. Same goes for the bathtub.'

'And most important, always put in a new roll of toilet paper before it runs out.'

'Amen,' said Gee Gee.

'Our next point of attack,' continued Tommy, 'is the living room. Why can't we keep it picked up — looking as if we're expecting company?'

'That's a good idea, Tommy,' said Gee Gee, 'but it may be too much to expect from all of us.'

'Yeah,' added Charlie. 'It's really not all that much of a mess; most of the time, it just looks lived-in, that's all.'

Gee Gee was sorry she had given Charlie an opening. She said, 'Let's not discourage Tommy. Let's give his plan a try. I'll still vacuum — and a lot more often, if you guys keep the place picked up.'

Tommy cut back in, 'Okay. No more newspapers, magazines, books, shoes, slippers, or games to be left scattered on the floor; or cluttered all over the couch or end tables. No more pretzel bags or beer bottles either — they're worth a nickel apiece now.'

'Great,' exclaimed Susan. 'Now I can invite friends over without first having to knock myself out for two hours picking up the place.'

She added, 'And I'll keep my own room looking like a show place.'

'Mine too — I'll do the same,' said Tommy.

'Good job. Guess that wraps it up,' said Charlie as he headed toward the fridge for a beer.

'Not so fast,' said Gee Gee. 'How about the garage — and the yard?

'Oh. No question,' replied Charlie. 'I get the message. They're mine. I'll keep everything shipshape.'

'Probably Chinese Junke,' said a little voice inside Gee Gee.

Charlie thought, 'Maybe this would be a good time to turn the lawn over to Tommy. He should do it anyway. Good for a kid to learn responsibility around the home.'

A $250,000 IDEA

What you have just witnessed is not really a miracle. Tommy has generated a lot of enthusiasm — but the world is filled with procrastinators who periodically have fits of resolution.

Will he pull this thing off?

I have a gut feeling that he will. But you understand if he does, his chances for becoming a SuperPRO will be virtually nil.

It looks to me as if Tommy Green is going to become one of those people who will use a system for GETTING

THINGS DONE — the system recommended by Ivy Lee — and for which one man voluntarily paid Lee $250,000.

I told about the system in one of my previous books, 'How To Make Money Writing and Selling Simple Information.' It has helped a lot of people who seem to have very little chance of being recognized for their ability as procrastinators.

I wouldn't tell you about it now, except an occassional person who reads this book may be like Tommy Green — Hell bent on getting things done.

One point needs to be clarified. The actual payment to Ivy Lee, many years ago, was $25,000. But if my math is anywhere near correct, that is the equivalent of a quarter of a million dollars in today's inflated currency.

Yep. That's correct.

Sometimes — not too often — But sometimes, even a procrastinator like me, uses the system which one man voluntarily paid $25,000 for. (in non-inflated dollars)

He paid it because it worked for him.

In fact, it helped him make one hundred million dollars ($100,000,000.00).

That was a long time ago. Yet, the same system still works for many of the most successful people in the world.

Maybe I better tell you about it.

His name was Charles M. Schwab. He first worked as a lowly stake driver for a steel company. Gradually, he worked his way up and finally became president of U.S. Steel.

Obviously he already was a very successful man, but he was not satisfied with his accomplishments. His was a tiny steel company — and he wanted it to grow big.

As luck would have it, a management consultant by the name of Ivy Lee, called on the company with a proposal which said his firm could help Mr. Schwab do a better job of managing.

Impatiently, Mr. Schwab said, 'Look, I don't want anyone helping me manage. But I will listen if you will just show me HOW-TO-DO-IT. And I will pay you anything within reason for the INFORMATION.'

Mr. Lee said, 'This is going to look like very, very SIMPLE INFORMATION. However, if you will use it, I am positive it will work.'

He handed Mr. Schwab a sheet of paper and a pencil, and said, 'Write down the six most important things you should do tomorrow.'

Mr. Schwab looked skeptically at Lee, but did as he was instructed. It took less than four minutes.

Then Mr. Lee said, 'Okay. Now number each of them in the order of their importance to you — and for the success of your company.'

Again Mr. Schwab did as instructed. It took more than twice as long to place them in 1,2,3,4,5,6,— order of importance.

Mr. Lee took the paper — looked at it — folded it — and said, 'Fine. Now put it in your pocket. When you arrive at work tomorrow morning, start working on item number 1. That is the one you selected as being MOST IMPORTANT to you and the profit of your company.'

'Stay with it until item one is completed.

'Don't let anything interfere.'

Mr. Schwab looked a little skeptical — was in fact skeptical.

So Mr. Lee said, 'If you let a lot of little things interrupt, you may get all of the little things done — and done well. BUT, the most important item will still be undone.'

'First things MUST come first.

'Then second, third, and so on down the list until you get your six most important things done. What you can't accomplish the first day, carry over to the second day.

'However, be dead sure each item is taken in the order of its importance. When all six are completed, you will be ready to make a new list of the MOST IMPORTANT items.'

Mr. Schwab said, 'It might work. What do I owe you?'

'Nothing,' replied Mr. Lee, 'until you prove its value to you and your company.

'Try it yourself.'

'Then have some of your key men try it, as long as you like.'

'When you are satisfied that this system will make money for you, pay me whatever you think it is worth to you.'

This entire consultation had taken less than half an hour. Yet, a few weeks later, Mr. Schwab had become so satisfied that he mailed Ivy Lee a check for $25,000 (an enormous consultation fee in those days.)

In his letter, Schwab said, 'Mr. Lee, this is the most profitable lesson — from a money making standpoint — that I have ever seen.'

In a relatively short time, Schwab's steel company was on its way to becoming the giant in the steel industry.

From a little guy — into a giant — all because of simple information — on a single sheet of paper. ONE IDEA - a very simple idea — listing things to do — in the order of their importance to you — and then doing them in THAT order.

That idea worked them.

It works today.

It will continue to work tomorrow — and for many more tomorrows.

Some of you will start using this idea immediately. But mark this guidebook — just in case you want to re-fresh your memory at some future date.

Things To Get Done!

	Date
1	
2	
3	
4	
5	
6	

However, BEWARE.

Do you have your membership card in PROcrastinators Club of North America?

Do you realize what might happen to you if you adopt the Ivy Lee system on a full time basis?

That's right.

As lifetime President, and chief executive officer of our exalted organization, I would be duty bound to ask you to surrender your membership card.

As a result you will deprive yourself of an opportunity to become a SuperPRO — at least until you mend your ways.

Reinstating yourself and obtaining a second membership card is not all that easy.

LIBRARY BOOKS

Please don't feel depressed it you lose your membership in Procrastinators Club of North America. We will still love you.

We will even encourage you as we carefully watch your progress in your new role as a totally success-oriented person.

It does not mean that our club has failed. There are always those who believe that the grass is greener on the other side of the fence.

You may be one of them, become weary of procrastinating, and decide to adopt a new lifestyle.

So be it.

More power to you.

We can always get new members. In fact, when forming new club chapters, we advise the founders to contact the local library for a list of preferred prospects.

They will be the people listed under 'past-due-books', people who never return a borrowed book on time. Their numbers are legion, and they can generally be depended upon to procrastinate on a lot of other things too.

A small city librarian told me, 'We have 1300 books seriously past-due — more than one year past due. We will wave all fines for the next two-weeks to get those books returned — or ask the borrower to pay half the cost of any missing book.'

Across the nation, past-due books are a tremendous problem. How big? Nobody knows. I tried to get centralized data for college, public, private, and high school libraries.

No one compiles nationwide figures.

That's just one more example of how difficult it is for procrastinators to get national recognition for their efforts.

Perhaps, more importantly, libraries should employ a method recently used by a Saratoga Springs Library. POLICE ARRESTS.

For a past-due book?

Yes. It can be — and is being used against those who completely ignore a long series of 'past-due' notices.

In New York state, it is a misdemeanor, subject to a $50.00 fine, or six months in jail.

What a wonderful opportunity to get a lot of reading done.

The Saratoga dragnet accomplished its mission. Many procrastinators outraced the police and got their books back to the library — posthaste.

Notable among those who didn't is a 19 year old student named (heck you don't need to know his name).

Records revealed he had borrowed four important books in 1982. It is now 1984.

When brought before the judge, he said, 'I've been meaning to take the books back, sir. But I never could find time to do it. I'm pretty busy.'

'TWO YEARS!', exclaimed the judged.

'My God, your honor. That's an awful stiff sentence. Why do I get TWO YEARS?'

'That's not a sentence,' replied the judge. 'That was a question — you are hereby fined $50.00. I hope you have learned your lesson. Case dismissed.'

The headquarters for Procrastinators Club of North America is appropriately located in a log cabin complex nestled in the foothills of the Adirondack Mountains of upstate New York.

Here on a woodland estate within the six million acre Adirondack State Park, the author finds peace and tranquility in great abundance — idyllic for a writer.

There are some inconveniences. I must walk or drive nearly two miles to pick up my daily mail at a rural mail box.

The Central Postmaster has declared our road 'unsafe' for the mail carrier. Yet the schoolbus picks up kids a mile or so up the road — UPS makes regular delivery — and polished cadillacs safely traverse to a private lake three miles beyond.

Would the giant US Postal Service willfully procrastinate about extending a rural mail route?

Otherwise, the postal service here is superior in every respect. The local Postmaster and her staff extend themselves daily to please everyone they serve.

They're great.

And no, she should not be called a Postmistress. The department does not recognize such a title.

UNFINISHED BUILDING

The man who built this log cabin and adjoining buildings is obviously a SuperPRO. Evidence is everywhere.

Take a look at it — judge for yourself.

The building is unusual in that it was constructed from old telephone poles. Every cedar log was first hand hewn with a broadaxe — then smoothed with a drawshave — a slow and tedious process.

The Maine Style construction requires that a quarter-cut log be inserted in the corner exterior uprights. He hasn't gotten around to doing it yet.

The building was erected in 1951.

The logs on three outer sides are in great shape — varnished as nicely as the hull of a pleasure boat. But the North side is weathered, dark — and attractive only to those who favor the old barnwood look.

He has been meaning to do something about it, but — well, you know how it is.

The fireplace mantle is not anchored, and should never be leaned upon. One eight inch piece of slate has yet to be installed in the hearth.

The knotty pine cathedral ceiling is complete except for six facings to hide the pink insulation where the tie logs meet the plates.

White wiring is showing beneath the picture window, where a baseboard has not yet been installed to anchor the electric heat unit, and to hide the wiring. That's understandable since the electric heat was not installed until 1969.

Most of the plumbing in the kitchen is hidden except for some copper pipes. However that will make it easier to get to them in case they ever spring a leak.

The exhaust unit over the corningware kitchen stove looks lovely, if you avoid noticing the seven inch gap in the chinking where the pipe exits through the logs.

During the summer months, we enjoy the mountain breezes on a large screened porch, totally oblivious to the fact that the rock foundation has not been completed at the north end.

Six perpendicular half-logs are also missing from the upper section at this end of the cabin. Why he favored the north end for postponed completion, is easy to understand. The embankment falls sharply away from the building at that point and it's a real pain in the butt to get to it.

AND, it is half hidden from view.

Moldings for the ceilings in the hallway and bedrooms are stacked neatly in one corner of the workshop, two car garage. None have ever been installed. I hesitate to install these myself. Might interfere with his plans.

Colonial trim for baseboards and window casements are in similar repose.

My wife is growing impatient about many of these minor details. To keep her happy, I periodically assure her that I will finish — or hire someone to complete the unfinished details of this building.

However, this kind of thinking is very disturbing to me. A contracted crash-program of completion would violate the legacy of a truly dedicated SuperPRO.

Why should I, or anyone else, desecrate the symbols of his enduring procrastination?

He is a retired senior citizen now, and is entitled to proper respect.

Sometime next week, or maybe the week after that, I'll try to find time to talk to him. I know exactly what he will say, 'Joe, I know how your wife feels. Tell her I won't put off that finishing work any longer. I'll get it all done just as soon as I can.'

I might as well be talking to myself.

That is the same promise he has made on each of the last seven occassions that I have talked with him. His guarantee is good enough to me.

I suppose, however, that it may no longer be wise for me to once again say to my dear wife, 'Dear, patience is a virtue. Give the man a little more time.'

However, I will point out to her how important it is to recognize that he is a man of 'good intentions'.

Or would you suggest a different course of action — perhaps something more tangible and immediate?

51

MY OWN BUSINESS

Are you one of those people who is forever saying, 'Someday, I'm going to have my own business; no more bosses; no more timeclock to punch; no more lousy commuting; and no more dead-end jobs.'?

It's the great American Dream, and paradoxically a very fertile field for developing procrastinator skills.

First decide you are going to operate a business from the privacy of your home. Brag about it a lot. But delay decision as to what kind of business to run.

Think about testing your business sense by selling someone else's product by mail. Answer all kinds of opportunity ads, but put off getting the feel of it on a part-time basis.

Decide to operate a beauty parlor; take an Adult Education refresher course in cosmotology; but postpone opening up a shop of your own until a more favorable time.

Consider making your own product and selling it wholesale to distributors. Check out the competition and market potential, but defer locating sources for raw materials and manufacturing equipment.

Make plans for converting the garage to a small repair shop; review 'How-to-fix-it' manuals; but wait until you think more people need things fixed before you set up shop.

Keep on fantasizing about all the money you can make by being in business for yourself; all the freedom and prestige you can have by being president of your own firm.

Hype up your enthusiasm; then cool off; postponement action on first one thing, then another. Defer getting in business for yourself and just become a leading contender for top honors in the field of procrastination.

It's easy.

SuperPROS AT COLLEGE

Those who are probably in greatest need for Time — most often — and sometimes in urgent need — are the SuperPROS found in the Hallowed Halls of learning on every campus across this great nation. The same is true in the seats of learning throughout the world.

Somewhere, somehow there may be an exception to this in some college that I have not heard about. I have been meaning to conduct a worldwide search for such a school but have not found time to so do — yet.

It matters not.

The important thing is that the need for Time is all pervasive in every college, academy, university, and any other center of learning known to humans.

Why is this true?

'Pure procrastination, the overwhelming omnipresence of procrastinators,' replied Dean Emory Pushmore.

The tone of his voice suggested that proacrastinators are akin to a plague.

I was really surprised to hear such a learned man take such an arbitrary stand.

Obviously he has never researched the great and continuing contribution that procrastinators make to our great economy, our society, and our culture.

To suddenly eliminate procrastinators from our society would create an economic disaster, panic, and financial chaos; the likes of which we have never seen before.

I am not ready yet to tell you why this is so. Furthermore, I have the feeling you are not yet ready to accept this fact. But, believe me, I plan on revealing this 'inside' information to you as soon as I can get to it.

Right now wouldn't you rather concern yourself with what happens on the college scene?

That is where some of the SuperPROS begin to develop their real finesse. Professors cannot publicly condone the accomplishments of dedicated procrastinators. However, they often privately marvel at the inventiveness and degree of imagination shown by some of the more capable practitioners.

In fact some professors have been known to appropriate several techniques not previously in their repertoire.

There is nothing so wrong about that. Isn't learning supposed to be a shared experience?

It certainly is!

Success Without College

And that may be one of the good reasons it is not necessary to go to college in order to become a SuperPRO.

Many a youngster is able to acquire all of the fundamentals of the art of praocrastination simply by observing the daily actions of his parents, his older brother, his sisters, and his Uncle Raymond—especially his uncle.

You see, Uncle Ray is the true patriarch of the local procrastinators. Everyone recognizes him for his uncanny abilityto get out of doing anything. Well almost anything. He does apply himself assiduously to eating and to drinking beer.

And he is a devoted baseball fan who has never been known to be late for a game. This last described action is inexcusable and would put a tarnish on his reputation in more sophisticated circles.

No world-class procrastinator is ever on time for anything. No never!

So if you are unable, unwilling, or even uninterested in going to college, be sure that you are careful who you use as a role model.

It would be counterproductive to find yourself emulating a 'week-end warrior' type of procrastinator. What you want is someone who has developed some meaningful skills in this field and applies them properly on a daily basis.

Having put your mind at ease that it is not mandatory to go to college to attain SuperPRO status, let's turn our attention to those who do follow that route. We will return to a less prestigious approach and its applications sometime later in this epistle.

Maybe some candid shots of our good friend, Hugh Allen Mattingale, III, will give us a closer look at the picture.

It is early morning at North Eastern.

Yes. It is very, very early morning and there is not the slightest glimmer of daylight to be seen through the crack in the bright orange drapes.

A piercing alarm clock shatters the rhythm of snoring and heavy breathing emerging from Room 12, (often discretely called 'Ham Haven'), on the third floor of Bellows Hall.

A voice grumbles, 'Jeez. What the Hell time is it?'

'3:30,' replies Hugh Allen Mattingale III as he snaps on the eye-stabbing light over his study desk.

'You dirty bastard,' exclaims a muffled voice from under the covers on the top bunk. 'What the Hell ya gonna do?'

'Finish my Chem II paper for my eight o'clock class.'

'What-da-ya-mean finish?' asks a heavy voice from across the room. 'Ya fat, lazy, no good slob, ya haven't even started yet.'

Hugh Allen Mattingale III was sensitive to being called "fat'. There was a hurt tone to his reply. 'That's not true. I just put it off until I got all my facts assembled. Sorta wanted to let it jell in my mind before I put it on paper. You know how it is.'

'Horseshit!'

'Anyway, I gotta get it typed up while the old juices are flowing.'

'Ya shoulda thought about that last night insteada using up all your juices going out with Miss Universe.'

'But I gotta —'

'No way, man! You start that typewriter and I'll heave your fat ass right out the window,' said Dick.

When Dick Simpson said something like that in the wee hours of the morning anyone with half a brain took heed. Why agitate a six-four 260 pound mean bundle of flesh?

It was easy for Hugh Allen Mattingale III to conclude, 'What the Hell. I'll get up at daylight and I can still get it typed if I press a little. Always work better under pressure anyway.'

If you are a serious student of the art of procrastination, you should be taking notes.

What did Hugh Allen Mattingale III do?

He recognized an opportunity to postpone doing an important piece of work until later. Plus he had one sleepy ear witness to testify that it was necessary for him to do so or suffer the dire consequences of being thrown out a third story window at 3:30 A.M..

What other choice did he have?

Sound rationale to support postponement of any action is vital to the success of even a rookie SuperPRO. Remember that!

Having scribbled that notation, let's get back to the scene of action.

It is now daylight. Bright and sunny, in fact. Hugh Allen Mattingale III reaches for the alarm clock and with one deft stroke silences the beastly thing — for the fifth time since dawn.

He mumbles, 'Jeez, I'm too goddamn tired. I can't even get my eyes open. How'n Hell can I see to type? I gotta get another fifteen. Then I'll wake up bright and cheery.'

Thus convinced, he resets the alarm for 15 (or something) and plops back into the half dream world of drinking and carousing with 'what's-her-name' last night.

'Man how could I have used up so much energy? I knew I had a paper to do. I did my bit fast. And I got in early. The relaxation was just what I needed to get ready to do my paper.'

Even in his sleepy state of semi-stupor Hugh Allen Mattingale III recognized that this kind of reasoning is fundamental in the world of procrastination. How else could one justify their action?

Hugh, or 'Ham the turd', as he was most often greeted by his fraternity brothers, had a tradition of family responsibility, dignity, and prominence to uphold. Certainly he would not do anything to blemish the family grace.

Someone of poor breeding might not have recognized the importance of being properly prepared before completing a Chem II paper. That individual might even have foregone the pleasures of preparation to which 'Ham the turd' had subjected himself last evening.

To what avail?

Certainly, Ham's paper would be equally acceptable to the ones produced by those lesser souls who hammered away most of the night in a state of nervous tension without the benefit of a pre-paper relaxation session.

It is true that the hour was fast approaching when the paper needed to be completed in its entirety. But anyone who is studying for a degree in procrastination has to know that putting things off until the last possible moment is fundamental to success.

What could be more exhilarating than to stand face to face with a compression chamber of urgency?

The Chem II paper must be done! Ham knows this.

It is simply a matter of complete concentration of one's mental faculties within a short time frame. A SuperPRO knows how to deal with this.

Ham was so convinced that he could handle the project within a lesser time frame that he decided it would be wrong to do anything other than to postpone the actual writing of the paper just a little bit longer.

Thus fortified, he wrapped himself in his blue terry-cloth robe, picked up his comb, soap, towel, toothbrush, D.O. stick, and headed down the hall to the frat's shower and fithouse. By the time he emerged he would be fit to be seen. Not idolized, but at least presentable.

Because time was growing short you might expect him to sort of rush through the morning toiletries. Not so!

Instead he proceeded to carefully layout his paraphernalia only to discover that he had forgotten his razor and shaving cream. This necessitated an unhurried trip down the hall and back. His movements in no way revealed that time was baring down on him. That is, not until Dick Simmons came hustling into the room.

'Get your fat ass oughta the way,' Dick said. 'What the hell you doin' hogging two spaces anyway?'

'I gotta lotta stuff,' he replied.

'What the hell are you still in here for anyway?' Dick asked. 'Weren't you all piss to start typing your paper at three this morning?'

'Yeah. And you made a big stink about it. Put me so far behind I don't know if I'm gonna be able to get it done in time.'

'Don't lay it on me, man! Just get your lazy ass in gear and get it done. It ain't gonna be good. But at least ya hand in something.'

Suddenly, without warning he grabbed all his crap. Tossed it in his wet towel. Made a mad dash down the hall to his room. Snapped a sheet of paper into his typewriter and began typing furiously. No notes.

One hour to go.

Anything he knew — and it wasn't much — was already in his head.

If there was one thing he did know, it was how to type. FAST. He had been a journalism major at Syracuse. A good one too. Expect for one thing. Deadlines! Too many other interesting things happening to keep up with the foolish deadlines imposed by a crackpot editor.

Transferring to North Eastern made a lot more sense. Who ever heard of a Research Chemist having to bust his ass to meet deadlines? A wise and considered move on Ham's part.

Of course, at this particular moment, Chem II was making some unfair demands on his time.

He erased all of these interfering thoughts from his mind. Like a man inspired, his fingers raced along the keyboard.

Complete concentration!

The answer to any procrastinator's prayer.

Somewhere, somehow his mind must have absorbed something on the subject. Because the keys kept spewing forth words, and more words. Not much rhyme, or reason, or structure.

However, fifty five minutes later, he had a paper. Fully typed.

He breathed a sigh of relief and raced for Sagamore Hall.

He didn't expect much of a mark.

Time passed. He and the class kept waiting and waiting for Prof Anderson to return the papers.

Prof explained, 'Sorry, but I have been unavoidably delayed.'

Weeks later, Ham finally did get his paper back. He read Prof A's one lonely notation. 'An interesting approach to the subject.'

Ham grinned, knowingly.

Yes, Ham passed, and at the top of the curve. Disparaging remarks by classmates were nothing — nothing more than envy for his brilliance and SuperPRO status.

What we have just witnessed is a mere tip of the iceberg of procrastination on the college scene. There's more. Lots more.

COMMUNITY COLLEGE

I have been meaning to find out if 'community colleges' are as common throughout the nation as they are in New York State. If you happen to know, please drop me a note — save me a lot of time.

These are the two year colleges which often serve residents of a one, two or three county area at reduced tuition rates. Some courses from these colleges are accepted as transfer credits by many four year colleges. With proper selection, students can get their freshman and sophomore years in and graduate to a higher center of learning as a college junior.

There are people who put off finding out if the college of their choice will accept these credits. They stand high on the procrastinator chart.

You may even know one or two of them.

Willie Hogan and Dan Fenton fit the category — to the point that classmates at ACC voted them 'the pair most likely to be late, late, late.'

Everybody loves Dan — he knows everyone in the school — has more charm than any movie star — and used it to override his otherwise unendurable tardiness. Willie clings to his coattails like Tonto.

They car-pool. They double date. They copy papers. They are inseparable.

Yesterday they tried to sneak into Prof Nelson's class late. No way. Prof says, 'OK, what made you guys late today?'

There is one thing about Hogan and Fenton that disturbs me. They are not purists in the field of procrastination. They are practitioners of what is better known as 'fashionably late.'

FASHIONABLY LATE

You know the type.

They are exploiters. They deliberately plan on being late — just to attract attention to themselves — with a grand entrance, gusto, maximized distraction, or what have you.

Is this true procrastination? I and a formidable body of SuperPROS say 'NO!' A few within the organization feel otherwise. The controversy rages on. At times it threatens to undermine the very foundations upon which the Procrastinators of North America have been so carefully built.

What do you think?

Perhaps reviewing some recent maneuvers by Hogan and Fenton will help you decide.

Yesterday, for instance, they burst into Prof Nelson's class late — and I do mean late.

Did they quietly sneak in and sit in the first available seats like any duly repentent tardy sinner?

Oh no! They made a grande entrance with Hogan loudly announcing, 'It's Fenton's fault we're late. He's driving.'

Fenton said, 'Wait a minute. I got to your place on time. But were you ready? No! You had to watch the last ten minutes of *Tom and Jerry* on your stupid TV.'

They repeated a slightly altered version of the same act for an afternoon class.

This time Hogan burst into Mechanics 203, red faced and puffing loudly. There was a long pause. You could hear Fenton in the hallway shouting amiably to everyone in sight like a politician on the campaign trail.

Prof J.C. Stepp continued fiddling with papers on his desk and sorting chalk as part of his five minute ritual of waiting for these two miscreants to arrive for class and to allow Fenton one last leisurely drag on his cig in the hallway.

Finally, Fenton strolled casually into the room as if it were his God-given right to keep everyone else waiting.

Hogan said, "Fenton was so wrapped up watching a football rehash that he lost track of time."

"Yeah. What about you?" asked Dan. "You had to get your last two-bits worth out of the arcade with Pac Man, Defender, and Tron. That gave us forty-two seconds to race across campus — rush up three flights of stairs — run the full length of two long hallways to get to Mech I on time. Hell, even O.J. couldn't do that."

Prof Stepp said, "I've had it with you guys. Don't pour out a profusion of excuses and apologies. We've heard them all before. Next time you're late, you better sneak in quietly or don't come at all."

Later in the day, the tardy twosome ran into Professor Nate Zimmerman of Calc III. He had a reputation for being diametrically opposed to anyone entering late and disturbing his classes. Up until now, he had tolerated their antics and late arrivals.

Today, he took great joy in watching the clock carefully for ten minutes until familiar voices could be heard coming down the hall. Then he non-chalantly crossed the room. Closed the door — locked it — turned his back to it just before Fenton piled into Hogan who had crashed into the locked door.

The prof's mischievous smile prevented him from seeing the noses pressed against the pane or from hearing the desperate pleading.

Hogan and Fenton gave up — retreated to the lounge to play pool and video — and thus assure being late for the next class.

Neither of them ever took decent notes in class, but always scrounged from diligent classmates. Hogan was brilliant and could pass from anyone's notes. Fenton could fail with an open book.

Looking....
FOR THE BEST

Zimmerman detested tardiness and poor study habits so much, he gave them one more whammy. As soon as everyone else had arrived on time for the final exam he said, "The exam site is room 301, up stairs. Please report there immediately."

Hogan and Fenton never found the site.

However, this did not eliminate them from graduating with the rest of the class.

It was not until the last possible moment — after everyone else was lined up and the line of march was moving — that these two strolled non-chalantly onto the scene gowns hanging open, caps in hand — late as always — but fashionably so.

I ask you. Are these guys worthy of recognition as dedicated procrastinators — or are they just showoffs?

Should they be classed with movie stars, pretentious socialites, politians, circus clowns, and race horses who wait until they are assured of an eager audience before making their appearance?

Procrastinators like to think they have become more sophisticated by the time they reach their junior year in college. For the sake of posterity and preservation of the species, let's hope that is true.

Would you like to see procrastinators become an endangered species?

Think of what it would do to our economy. I will tell you a little later in this book — if I get around tuit.

Right now, let's listen to Kathy and Stan, lab partners in Chem II.

'But, Kathy, if I'm going to understand this procedure, you gotta tell me what's been done to this point'? 'Look man, I'm tired of coming in here ten minutes early to get the lab all set up so you can waltz in fifteen minutes late and expect me to do all your work for you.'

'Sorry, Kathy, but I overslept.'

'Why? Because of Happy Hour? Or were you watching Dynasty or Johnny Carson last night? You look like death warmed over.'

'You know how to hurt a guy. Sometimes I get unexpectedly delayed.'

'Not just sometimes. You're always late for everything. What are you going to tell Prof Hess? . . . you overslept . . . you forgot to warm up the car . . . your books weren't ready . . . you couldn't find your lab writeup . . . your roomy is sick and you had to go to the drug store to get him medicine . . . you lost track of time doing research in the library . . . you forgot it was Wednesday?'

'No,' replied Stan. 'I'm the one who's sick. I probably shouldn't even be here.'

'Then why don't you go to the john . . . get a drink of water . . . write something in your agenda book . . . sharpen your pencil? You know — your standard routine before your settle down to doing anything that remotely relates to the lab project.'

'Okay. Let's discuss it later. It's almost break time. Guess I'll get a cuppa coffee. Better dash next door to the bakery for some doughnuts first.'

'Don't forget to spend an extra ten minutes chatting with Sarabelle. Then you'll only have forty five minutes of lab time left. How did I get you for a lab partner, anyway?'

'Just lucky, Kathy. Just lucky.'

In a way, Kathy was lucky. Stan was a near genius in the lab — once he got his ass in gear. That never occurred until the night before the lab write-up was due.

Kathy found that out when she phones Stan for help on a problem after working all weekend on the thirty page work-up.

Stan said, 'Wow. You can't be that far already. I haven't started yet. I may — and probably will get on it and give you a call back tonight.'

He never did.

But come Tuesday night, Kathy's phone rang. 'Hi, partner. How about going over that lab stuff tonight to be sure we're on the right track?'

'Okay. If it won't take too long. I'm beat.'

Ten minutes later Kathy appeared at his door. Project in hand, knowing it would be easier to escape his place than to get rid of him at hers.

'My God, Stan,' she said. 'You got a ton of books and papers spread all over the joint. Where do you want to start?'

'Instrumental Analysis.'

'That means you haven't even started yet.'

'I've been meaning to. But I've been busy,' replied Stan.

'Sure you have. What are you majoring in — popularity? Do you ever miss parties, pub nights, beer blasts, or any social event of any kind — or pass up any chance to shoot the breeze? No. And on top of that you're president of the Science Club, and work at the gold club. You're nuts. When do you expect to get any school work done?'

'Right now. Let's go.'

Kathy marveled. Under pressure, Stan became a model of proficiency. No whipping it off just to get it done. No sir.

He had to know how to calculate every standard deviation, not with a calculator — but by hand, in case he punched a wrong button. He was exacting, precise, and intolerant of the slightest ambiguity. A most noble approach. But with so few hours left, it seemed ridiculous.

Nevertheless, this previous master of dilly-dally became a paragon research scholar. It mattered not to him that his lab partner was bleary eyed and ready for bed.

His term paper went the same way.

He said, 'Kathy, I can't find enough on my subject here at SUNY TECH. Library's too meager. I'm ordering stuff on inter-library loan.'

'But, Stan, that's a three week delay. You got wheels. Why not hit some of the other three nearby college libraries?'

'Inter-loan is more convenient.'

'I know. Means you can put off doing anything 'til the stuff gets here.'

When the material finally arrived, Stan was unhappy. 'Insufficient, inadequate, inappropriate,' Stan said. 'I'll change my topic.'

'You don't have time,' complained Kathy.

'Sure I do. We got a college computer. I'll use its Lit Research capabilities.'

Four days in a row he tried to access it. 'It's jammed, Kathy. I can't get anywhere. I still got three weeks and two days to get all the data I need. I'll write away for stuff and hit the local libraries.'

During the next couple of weeks, Stan amassed a formidable pile of articles, Books and computer print-outs. Intimidating in its scope.

Kathy asked, 'How's it coming?'

'Great. Soon as it's all here, I'll organize it and get going. Still got 'til next Tuesday. I got other things to get out of the way first. Then I can concentrate fully on the paper.'

'No time like the present,' said Kathy.

'I agree. Right after I go to Bob's birthday party — make some calls for the Science Club's Christmas Party, and . . .'

'You're nuts, Stan. Just plain nuts.'

By Monday, he appeared frantic, grouchy, short-tempered — and in BIG trouble.

He said, 'All I got left to do is the cover page, bibliography, illustrations,and six or seven more pages of text. And get it to a typist by 3:00 p.m.'

He delivered it to the furious typist at 10:00 p.m. — not proof read — not page numbered — not recopied — arrows and inserts everywhere. But he had it done!

An hour before class, the next morning, Stan was racing to correct mistakes in the final typed copy — misspellings — improper deletions of important text — illustrations missing — and entire sections typed in the wrong sequence.

Stan said, 'Boy, I'll never take any work to that typist again!'

Have you been paying close attention to Stan's procrastination technique?

If so, be sure to carefully evaluate your cabilities before you attempt to emulate him. Are you brilliant? Do you like to work under extreme pressure? Are you immune to ulcers? Are you able to charm others into accepting your dilatoriness?

Did you answer YES — to all four questions?

Really?

Okay. Then you have the makings of a SuperPRO. Go for it.

THUMBS UP!

IN THE WONDERFUL WORLD OF WORK

Perhaps it's time we tested some of our precepts in the land of reality . . . the workplace.

Entry into that Haven of Happiness has its beginnings sooner than most of us think.

In our dreams, I would guess. When we are kids.

What did you dream of becoming?

Someday!

Did you explore beyond the world of dreams and say to yourself, 'I want to. Yes, I intend to become a (_____).'

Good!

Now we have the basis on which to build a career. Or at least get started.

YOUR CAREER

Having set a goal of becoming (let's say) an accountant, is a very good move on your part. Much better than just drifting along aimlessly. Besides it is now evident that you 'have good intentions.'

Since you are still in school, you are advised to take all the Math courses you possibly can. Math is easy for you anyway, so you decide to delay Bookkeeping II until after you have had a chance to expose yourself to Woodshop II.

Most college-bound students take only a year of Woodshop not realizing that it will be impossible to take any advanced studies in this craft unless you go to a trade school or come back for evening Adult Ed courses.

Besides, in Woodshop you can end up with tangible evidence of your skills; good or even excellent replicas of period furniture which will last a lifetime. Things your parents can point to with pride and say 'See, that's what Tommy made for us in his junior year.'

You are justly proud.

And there is nothing wrong with that. Why not take advantage of an opportunity to learn, have fun, and be productive all at the same time?

Your math education will not be totally 'on hold.' After all, attention to detail and precise mathematical measurements are required in order to produce superior pieces of furniture. Accountants must learn to be precise.

You know full well that you will take Bookkeeping II as soon as you can get to it. As an A+ student, you are already assured of enough credits, plus high scoring in your SATs to get you into college.

What difference will it make that you fall a bit short of the entry requirements at the most prestigious accounting college in the nation?

There are other accounting schools that will be happy to admit Tom. One in Boston, one in Chicago, and others elsewhere. Their graduates get jobs — maybe not at the same level as for grads from the top three. But they do get jobs.

WOODWORKING

RATIONALIZING!

Why not? It is surely a fundamental tenant for anyone worthy of being considered as a budding, young procrastinator. Use it.

Why should it matter to Tom that his friend Leo would be accepted at Princeton? Leo was just one of those B students who never let anything deter him from his designated target. Pitiful.

SuperPROS AT WORK

JOB HUNTING

You obviously know that the logical next step after getting an education is to go 'job hunting.'

Hunting is a sport.

It truly fascinates millions of Americans, both male and female. Generally a hunting license is required. But not for males hunting females or for females hunting males.

Can't understand how the tax people ever overlooked this one. The revenue from licensing this one sport could eliminate the national debt in a matter of months.

However, we should not concern ourselves about that at the moment. Right now we must focus our attention on the various techniques of getting a job; more commonly referred to as Job Hunting.

In particular, we are most concerned about the techniques employed by various unemployed individuals whose intentions are good. They really want to, or have to, get a new job.

Walter A. Sawyer, (whoops) Walter A.S. is one of them. Yet he is also working on becoming a SuperPRO. These two diametrically opposed objectives can cause a bit of a conflict.

Walter is a graduate of Harvard, a very prestigious school indeed. He matriculated in Business Administration. He is known to have cut a class or two. Well, maybe several. But he never missed a beer bust.

Graduating from five years at Harvard may have helped him get a job in the Trust Division of a New York City bank despite the fact that his father was prominent on Wall Street and a member of the bank's Board of Directors.

He was socially very gracious, and picked up a substantial number of accounts from connections developed on the cocktail circuit. His clients were mostly those with an affinity for 'growth stocks.' They completely overlooked the possibility of any exchange of 'insider' information from his father. They just plain liked the handsome, debonair 'new man at the bank' who was so shrewd at investing their funds.

They prospered. The bank prospered. He prospered.

Within months Walter became a vice-president. A most unheard of accomplishment for anyone who had started at the bottom of the Trust Department ladder such a short time ago.

Since Walter had proven to be such a superior salesman, the bank decided to utilize his talents in a broader field. He 'hit the road' to pick up business from an ever increasing number of banks in the great Northeast.

He wined and dined prospective bankers lavishly. They loved him.

Not much time had passed when a mid-size bank in a small city not too far from Boston spotted him. 'The perfect man to replace Fred Farley when he retired as President two years from now,' proclaimed Board Chairman Kelso.

They hired him.

No one questioned the effusive commendations from the New York City bank. Neither did they wonder why the New York bank had not made counter offers to try to hold such an obviously valuable man.

Only three members of the mid-size bank were aware that Board member Paul I. Gills had aspirations for the presidency.

Walter took the title of assistant vice president so as not to reveal the real reason for his entry into the bank. Standard procedure of confidentiality in many a small city.

He made a very favorable impression on the elite of the community. Everyone who was anyone invited him to their parties. He never missed a cocktail party or a happy hour. Even those thrown by lesser lights in the surrounding towns.

He was it.

They soon made him a Vice-president.

Everyone liked and respected him. Except the 'subordinates' who worked under him. This, however, was not true of buxom Vera Downs. She enjoyed working under a domineering, autocratic, virile man. Or as far as that was concerned, under any man.

As his personal secretary, Vera Downs tried to protect him. She was well versed in the philosophy of PYA.

One day she said, 'I think I should warn you about that tonic bottle in your bottom drawer. If certain members of the Board found out about it you would be in big trouble.'

Arrogantly he replied, 'So what will they do about it? I'm a full Vice-president. They certainly are not going to fire me. Besides it's in a clearly marked cough syrup bottle. Who's to know the difference?'

He paused and said, 'You bitch! You been nipping on it, haven't you?'

That was a mistake. Vera Downs did not like to be accused of nipping on anybody's bottle. No way!

Three months later, the bank announced, 'Paul I. Gills, a long and respected member of our Board of Directors has been elected to a newly created position of Senior Executive President. He will assume the duties of Bank President during the next five months while President Fred Farley is on an extended vacation prior to his mandatory retirement in November.'

It was a long hot summer for you-know-who. Vice-presidents DO get fired. Walter found that out in mid-December.

I hope you don't think I am deliberately postponing telling you about the techniques used by procrastinators when job hunting.

Heavens no!

You may be in dire need of this body of knowledge sometime in your own future. Why should I deprive you of information which may someday be of considerable value to you? That is, if you put it to good use.

It seems advisable to give you a little background about Walter A.S. If you are to understand his necessity, or possibly desire to go job hunting.

Would you be satisfied if I only told you, 'Walter had a job. He got another job. He drank on the job. He was fired. Now he has to hunt for his third job.'?

Heck no!

You are entitled to know WHY he is job hunting.

Problably I should also tell you that he has two sons, two daughters and on wife. This might have a bearing on how he goes about it.

In fairness to Paul I. Gills, let me point out that he gave Walter an opportunity to enroll in AA and straighten himself out and retain his position as a Vice-president. Gills was not the kind of man his initials might suggest.

Walter did not. Instead, his arrogance flourished.

He was given four months severance pay. No letter of recommendation. Seemed odd.

Thus insulated against starvation, Walter did not look for a job, or position, as he would call it. Why should he? By now the word was out. He was available. THEY would come hunting him.

Two months went by. THEY did not come. Unbelievable.

Boston was not that far away. He could commute. He decided to call some former classmates now comfortably employed in banks or brokerage houses in Bean Town.

Cal said,'Yea, old buddy. I heard. Wish my old man had something open for you. We sure would like to have you aboard. Hate to postpone hiring you. Bill Jones might have something right now. Why don't you give him a jingle?'

He did.

Bill's secretary answered. 'Sorry. Mr. Jones is in Bermuda on a month's vacation. Could someone else help?'

'No thanks. I'll call when he returns.'

Now conditions were ideal. Exactly what a confirmed procrastinator needs.In this case an INTENT could not be activated until Bill returned. There was sound reason to delay any further action.

He was convinced that was the place he wanted to work. Why hunt elsewhere?

It is important to have convictions if you are to develop any meaningful degree of expertise in procrastination.

Convinced as he was, Walter developed a bit of uncertainty after two weeks of waiting. He said, 'It might be best to improve my odds. I might even want to return to New York. I could write a couple of pals there.

He did.

Not much different really than betting on two horses in the same race. Despite your conviction, your favorite horse sometimes loses.

Would you believe that?

I hope so. Because it has been known to happen.

At least once or twice.

Every day.

Walter expected prompt and courteous replies. He got them. Charlie said, 'Sorry, old boy. Nothing here at the moment. Suggest you give Chase or Hanover a try.'

Pat's reply said, 'Sorry, my friend, we have nothing now. Why not get in touch with Charlie?'

Walt was no dummy. He got the picture.

It was fast becoming all too apparent that the kind of position he was seeking was 'not available' right now.

Did that give him reason to delay any aggressive job hunting action? Sure did.

Now he had evidence that it would be wiser to put it off until conditions were right. Besides, he was beginning to lose a bit of confidence. Not much, but some. And that can breed fear.

It worked for Walter A.S.

He could have said, 'I've got a lot of contacts out there. If I get in touch with enough of them, someone will give me a crack at a new position. That kind of job hunting should be fun.'

But the looming specter of possible rejection and defeat was too much for Walt. It was entirely foreign to his lifestyle. He had never before been confronted with this kind of dilemma. He didn't really know how to handle it.

Contrary to his normal arrogant nature, he backed off. He made no phone calls, wrote no letters, sent no resumés.

No more job hunting of any kind.

He was on a fast downhill course heading for a crash landing.

It worked.

No leads. No offers. No job in sight.

His severance pay was running out. He decided he would have to apply for unemployment insurance. But not right now. It could wait a little while longer.

But his wife could not. She and the kids left him. His dilatory tactics were gaining him a lot of points toward SuperPRO.

Had it not been for a more experienced contender, he would have made SuperPRO of the week. His chances were still good for the following week.

But he blew it.

He made phone calls. He wrote letters. He mailed out resumés. He even scoured the classifieds.

His hunting paid off. He got a job.

A used car salesman. Not in his league. But a job nevertheless. His family returned.

HANDLING A JOB INTERVIEW

While we are on the subject of jobs, let's move into the area of The Interview.'

This is a direct quote from H.A. 'Buzz' Bezanson in his valuable book, 'How To Successfully Win Job Interviews.'

If you want a copy, send me a stamped, self-addressed envelope and I'll tell you where you can get a copy.

Marion O. Mason has been through the interview process before and knows that it can be a nerve wracking experience. She has good credentials, good work experience, and good looks.

For some time now, she has been meaning to re-enter the job market. She sends out a perfectly prepared resumé to three fine area firms.

Apparently she has exactly the right qualifications. All three firms book her for an interview on the same day. Not the best arrangement, but the timing looks just right so she can squeeze them all in and get it over with in one day. She calls each firm to confirm that she will be there at the specified time.

She intended to look up information about each firm. That way she would be able to show each interviewer how interested she was in their firm.

However, she had the makings of a SuperPRO and said, 'I just can't seem to find time to do it. I'll wing it.'

The more practice one has at being tardy, the better one becomes at winging it. Marion was good.

She arrived at her first destination a good ten minutes early. This gave her time enough to look around to observe the general character of the people working at this office.

But she felt time could be better spent re-doing one of her nails. She could check the staff out sometime in the future.

As if making small talk, she asked the receptionist, 'Will Ms Jones be interviewing me?'

We don't have a Ms Jones. Mr. Blake, our new interviewer, will be talking with you soon.'

The word 'mister' made her suddenly realize she had deferred putting on a dash of Chanel Number Five. She whipped a little bottle from her purse and splashed. Too fast and too much.

Oh well, she thought. A little overpowering with a man is okay. And if he is new at interviewing, he is bound to be very nervous anyway.

This will do him good.

It pleased her to know that her tardy action would work in her favor.

My, oh my. How wrong she was.

He had just been divorced by a Chanel Number Five wife. He was now into Musk.

Within a couple of minutes she sensed the negative vibes. She, of course, did not know what was causing them, but they were there.

It was not in her best interest to prolong the agony. She knew it. Why let herself get all worked up and spoil her chances at the next two interviews?

There was an easy way out. She said, 'Mr. Blake, I must confess I was planning to be ready for this interview. But I got side tracked. Do you think it would be better for me to wait until I am fully prepared? Then come back?'

'Yes, Mrs. Marion', he said. 'That is very good thinking. We will call you when we have another opening.'

'Just one more thing,' she said. 'The resumé I mailed in wasn't exactly complete. I meant to, but didn't have time to check it over carefully.'

She shuffled through her blue handbag. Pulled out three sheets of paper. Handed them to him and said, 'Here this should just about complete my file.'

He said, 'Thanks.' But somehow FAILED to convey sincerity.

She left the office determined to go directly to the Chamber of Commerce. She now had some free time. She could use it to look up information about her next prospective employer.

This is a perfectly acceptable procedure for a SuperPRO candidate. Why? You know why. Waiting until almost the last possible moment to accomplish a planned task is a classic maneuver for procrastinators.

However, Marion bumped into her friend Elsie. This gave her an opportunity to once more postpone the look-up assignment. Each postponement gives a SuperPRO candidate some additional points.

Marion got them.

She went to lunch with Elsie. A nice long two-hour lunch. Two, or possible three martinis.

When she arrived at Hutton's she was already ten minutes late for the interview. She had hurried and was out of breath, puffing hard. That should convince them she had been unavoidably delayed.

It did not.

But it did spew her breath forcefully under the large nose of Ms Stepp, her rather elderly interviewer. Rule number 12 prevailed and the interview was over.

The quickness with which these interviews were being completed was costing Marion points on the SuperPRO score charts.

Quickies are frowned upon.

She contemplated skipping the final interview of the day. 'I simply won't show up,' she said. Complete failure to show would have given her several points.

Nevertheless, she decided to forsake such easily gotten gains.

She was loaded.

During the interval between interview number two and interview number three, she regrouped her plans and developed a pleasing new strategy.

She would take the inititative.

She did.

Before the final interviewer could make some snide remark about her hair, Marion said, 'I know my hair is not freshly permed. I planned to get it done but ran out of time.'

'We know how that is on such short notice,' smiled Ms Lippencott.

'Besides, my last boss was such a slob, she never cared. Marion continued, 'Whenever she felt like getting dolled up, she got on everybody's back. Tried to get along with her and the mangy bunch of cats who worked there. I finally quit.'

'I notice you had four previous jobs.'

'Oh I had lots more. Why make you check all over town? Four gives you enough variety so you can see I'm willing to do anything. Besides I was in a hurry when I typed up my resumé.'

'Well now,' said Ms Lippencott

Marion interrupted. 'My references may act a little surprised when you call. There wasn't time for me to get in touch with them first.'

'But —'

'Anyway all you want to know is what kind of worker I am. I am systematic. I am willing to follow instructions unless you don't allow enough time to get the work done on time. Then I take shortcuts.'

'We wouldn't —'

'What's more, I am very prompt. I leave work promptly at quitting time. There's always time to finish it the next day.

'I am a well rounded person. I have my own life to lead. I am not one of these goody-two-shoes who gets all wrapped up in community affairs. I devote all of my work effort to my employer.

'I expect to be properly paid for it too,' said Marion.

Without pausing she added, 'By the way, how good are your benefits? I hope you are not one of those strict old biddies who is going to demand a note from the doctor any time I am out sick. Furthermore, I don't expect somebody to jump on my back in case I'm ten or twenty minutes late once in awhile in the morning.

'I got enough problems as it is. And the doctor wants me to get more sleep. If I could get my housework done sooner, I could go to bed earlier.'

'Well, young lady,' said Ms Lippencott as she rose to conclude the interview, 'You have certainly told me all I need to know.'

FOR THOSE OF YOU who are intent on developing your skills as a procrastinator, notice how easy it is to weave key phrases into any conversation so as to let any one see clearly where you stand.

It's about time I told you HOW TO QUALIFY to have your name and picture placed in the SuperPRO HALLOWED HALL OF HESITATION (which as I told you before is the HALL OF FAME for those who distinquish themselves as the BEST PROCRASTINATOR in their field).

1. Be able to prove you have developed a unique method of putting things off — in some segment of your life.

2. You must reveal how you justify your actions to your spouse, your boss, your team-mates, or other colleagues.

3. Be willing and able to explain your exploits clearly and concisely.

4. Creativity is important. So is longstanding success.

5. Two reliable witnesses must sign your entry form to assure the judges that you are a reliable procrastinator; one who can be depended upon to NOT get things done — on time, in a particular category.

To obtain an official entry form and complete instructions SEND a long self-addressed, stamped envelope to:

SuperPRO
Entry Form
711 Lake Nebo Road
Fort Ann, NY 12827

Any time you get around to it.

...A WORLD OF OPPORTUNITIES.

BEHIND THE SCENES IN BUSINESS

Trying to get behind the scenes in today's business world is a very difficult task. There exists a paper jungle which is almost impenetrable for even the most persistent investigative reporters.

Which ones would you expect to be the most difficult in which to get behind the scenes?

You're right.

Banks, high tech, illicit drugs, and munitions factories head the list.

Government offices do not count. We are looking for businesses that can survive only if they make a profit.

Since you thought of banks first, would you like to try our luck there?

Banks are at the very hub of ALL — yes ALL business. If you don't believe this is true, show me a business that exists without using a bank in some form or other.

So if we break our way into the inner recesses of a bank, what will we find?

Money!

Sure. But let's look for something more practical.

Will we find SuperPROS?

Yes we will.

All we need do is spend some well invested time observing the actions of a variety of people we encounter within one of these palatial profit centers.

HIDING WITHIN A BANK

A giant bank would be better. But let's settle for a 600 million dollar bank in a prosperous city in upstate New York.

Our research team found 407 people on staff. That is a sufficient number from which to obtain a valid sampling of seasoned procrastinators.

To the untrained eye, it might appear that all of them are panning for gold. Your gold.

That simply is not so.

Some of them are living legends of the bank's slogan. YOUR MONEY IS SAFE WITH US.

They are the bank tellers; 127 smiling faces at lobby windows in the main downtown office, branch offices, walk-up, and drive-in windows throughout the bank's four-county domain.

To you, these people are known as bank tellers. But within the bank, a concerted effort is being made to identify them more properly as CSR's.

The bank's Public Relation Department has combined forces with the Personnel Dept. in a courageous effort to sell this fine new identity to the public and to the old die-hards within the bank.

How much easier it would be for the average customer to proudly say, 'I'm going to have a Consumer Service Representative cash my check.'

But they don't. do you suppose customers are putting it off until the time is right?

Customers have procrastination rights too, you know.

THE PUBLIC RELATIONS MAN

Would you like to take a good look at the bank's PR man?

No one would suspect Carl A. Williamson of being a procrastinator. He is gregarious, outgoing, and very, very persuasive.

That's his job. Sell. Sell. Sell.

He is constantly on the go promoting the bank's image in every segment of every community served by his bank.

Carl exudes warmth and charm. He knows a tremendous number of people by their first names. He is a compulsive name dropper and claims to know thousands more, especially those in high places.

That's okay.

As Vice-president of Marketing, Public Relations, and Advertising — he should.

Of all the people on the staff, he should be best at capturing large new accounts and 'closing the sale'.

Paradoxically, he is not.

He is forever waiting for more favorable conditions. When he runs up against resistance, he waffles. He will immediately switch sides of an argument without seeming to be aware that he is doing so.

He gets himself so involved in joining organizations and social activities that he is forever postponing projects which might very well be more beneficial to the bank.

He gains lots of SuperPRO credits without even trying.

THE BANK COMPTROLLER

Orville Killington, is the man responsible for the general ledger, the central records of the bank's assets and liabilities.

He is very practical and pragmatic. Strictly a no nonsence guy. To him, figures are romance. Not the kind of figures we normally associate with romance. He loves those that dance through computer printouts.

His life is very structured, orderly, and carefully maintained along established work patterns.

No one can intimidate him into rushing reports out before he has carefully checked them to assure their accuracy. He does not dilly-dally and delay. He simply maintains a slow and deliberate pace.

Unike the Public Relations executive, he is happy to maintain a relatively small circle of friends. He considers them to be close and intimate associates. No phonies.

When new methods are proposed, he will stall, delay, and do all he can to postpone the inevitable. Otherwise, he is very inept at procrastinating. Count him out.

THE BANK MAILBOY

It is hard for me to understand why this employee is still referred to as a 'mail boy'. He has been on the staff for nearly ten years now, and will be thirty years old in late October.

I hope the Public Relations people get around to giving him a more sophisticated title in the near future.

Look at him.

He carries a heavy load. Were he on the executive staff, he would be known as a specialist. In truth, that is what he really is. He is as devoted to his narrow line of work as is the bank's Investment Officer.

People like him. He is a considerate, modest individual who is always willing to help those he considers to be his friends. He loves his familiar work environment with its predictable work pattern.

Mortimer Albert Noonan is his name.

Some people in Personnel accuse Mort of not working up to his potential. They claim he makes excellent grades on periodic tests.

When cajoled, he signs up for 'staff improvement' classes. He out scores everyone in the first semester exams. Then he cannot seem to find time to attend many of the remaining sessions.

Once Mort discovers there is no real challenge to a course of study, he finds a dozen or more reasons for not completing the course.

To himself, he says, 'Any fool can learn that stuff I'm going to wait until something really difficult comes along. Then I won't be wasting my time.' He is right — especially about the first part.

He is also wrong.

How can learning something — anything, be a waste of time?

Mort should know that the more wasted time he can accumulate, the better his chances will become for SuperPRO. He already has accumulated an enviable number of points by simply never taking the initiative in anything. He is always content to wait for orders before acting.

A recent Secretary of State could have learned a lot from Mort.

THE PERSONNEL EMPIRE

The power vested in Upstate National Bank's Vice-president of Human Resources and Personnel is awesome.

She is Caroline Angel Titsworth - close and trustworthy ally of President Grimes.

She can hire.

She can fire.

She can make promotions; or veto suggested promotions.

She can approve or disallow salary increases: or can cause salary decreases.

She can override any other Vice-president or division head in their selection or placement of personnel.

She can and does see to it that staff members are penalized for tardiness, excessive personal use of bank phones, gum chewing, any negative attitude, or sexual harassment. Males only.

Did you hear that devastating blonde Trudy Bennett?

Trudy said, right in the presence of a group of bank officers in the main lobby, 'Harass me, fellas. Harass me. I love it.'

Oh yes she did.

How many of them will report same to Ms. Titsworth? None!

How could that be?

Ms. Titsworth is also responsible for the Bank's dress code. Very prim and proper attire is essential to maintain a suitable public image.

She wrote the policy. She PO-lices it.

She can con the Board of Directors into accepting and authorizing virtually any policy that even remotely relates to bank personnel.

How did she gain such great stature?

Two years ago she saved the bank money. $150,000 of it.

She had been with the bank only about a year as Human Resources Person. Yet she was able to convince the EEO that the bank did not have evil intentions. Any discrimination had been purely unintentional.

She produced written policies and guidelines designed to guarantee equal opportunity and upward mobility for women. She argued that the bank had not yet had time to put the program into effect. The Federal government conceded. Their $300,000 claim against the bank was cut in half.

No one questioned as to who had blown the whistle to EEO in the first place; or how the EEO inspector was able to locate the most incriminating files within Personnel in a matter of minutes. Ms Titsworth was immediately promoted. She became a Vice-president one day before her 40th birthday.

Sincerely appearing to be sincere is an art. She has mastered it. Ms Titsworth can't seem to do enough to help others. She spearheads many community affairs. She is pictured often in the local newspaper.

At the bank, the personnel files have taken on a new look. They are jam-packed with reports and documentation of every kind concerning each employee.

She has secret files too. They would put J. Edgar Hoover to shame.

She believes in rules, regulations, and reports. They abound.

Her empathy for people is studied and ostentatious. Her suspicions are hidden.

She would make an excellent auditor.

Or an FBI sting agent.

Or a CIA clandestine operator.

Or a Russian general in Warsaw.

What does she know about bank president Hudson Osmond Grimes?

Who would think it possible for such a dynamic individual as Ms. Titsworth to procrastinate?

Her elderly mother does.

Just the other day, mother phoned and said, 'But Caroline, the last five times I have called, you promised to come see me sometime very soon. It's only a forty-five minute drive to the nursing home.'

'I know Mother. I promise you I'll try to get there sometime next week.'

That very same evening she said to her daughter Pam, 'I'm sorry honey. I can't go to your class play Friday night. Something's come up at the bank that I must attend. I'll be sure to go to the next school affair.'

'That's great. Daddy gave up his poker game to come see me. And he cancelled his fishing trip to go see Teddy play Little League. But not you. You always put us off until the next time.'

'Now see here, young lady.'

Pam stormed out of the room in tears.

Later that evening, Caroline said, 'Not tonight Tom. Let's wait until I feel in the mood'

That last refusal can pick up a lot of SuperPRO points. It is fraught with danger.

It takes courage.

It can mean disaster. But some people will risk anything to increase their chances for entry into the SuperPRO Hallowed Hall of Hesitation.

BRANCH ADMINISTRATOR

Henry E. Densmore, is the VP in charge of twenty nine branch offices.

He is good. He is knowledgeable. None know or care for his people the way he does. Hank is always willing to plunge into deep water on their behalf — especially if it entails a confrontation with Ms Titsworth.

His ability to manage work and people for a profit keeps him in the good graces of the Board of Directors. Not only is he aggressive he is persuasive and knows how to harness people to help him reach his goals.

He hates interference from anyone in the Personnnel department. His people know this and love him for it.

Maybe it's his hate for Personnel Policies that causes him to procrastinate so profoundly.

I don't know.

I do know that hostility can be an underlying reason for procrastinating. And if that is what it takes, he's got it.

For instance: his semi-annual formal, Performance Review reports are seldom delivered on time.

He hates formality. He prefers to deal with his people on a one-to-one basis. No two are alike.

Last winter he said, 'Marie, you are doing a terrific job with your loans. Keep it up.'

At another branch,he said, 'Joe, you gotta drag your ass -get out there and get more deposits.'

Marie made more loans than any other branch office during the next three months. Deposits increased substantially at Joe's branch. Such results convinced Densmore that his method was best.

'Listen,' he said to each of his people 'We gotta go through this formal crap. You already know how you're doing. But I still have to file a stupid report with Personnel.

'I put off doing it as long as I could. Titsworth will castrate me if it's not in by tomorrow.'

On board ship that would be mutiny.

Even in the bank, it could be cause for dismissal.

Like many procrastinators, Densmore had little time for details. 'This is meaningless crap,' he said. 'What I look for is bottom line results. Why try to make everybody perfect? Gets you nowhere.'

SENIOR LOAN OFFICER

Any man who holds the job of Senior Loan Officer in a bank is out of his everloving mind - or soon will be.

If the loan portfolio is in top shape, the Board and the National Bank Examiners will say, 'Well that's the way it's supposed to be.'

On the other hand, if several loans are to be charged off, they ask, 'what idiot permitted these loans to go through in the first place?'

Banks fail — or are forced to merge with a larger bank because of a lousy loan portfolio.

Guess whose head is on the chopping block?

Knowing that, you can now understand why FEAR is what drives a Senior Loan VP like Ronald A. Manchester.

Could that be why he has an ulcer?

And why he is so painstaking in maintaining high loan standards.

His paperwork is horrendous. The top of his desk looks like a bargain basement sales counter.

Each pile of paper has its own special place and meaning.

1. Hold until later.
2. Defer -get more info.
3. Withhold approval - unless forced.
4. Delay - customer may get tired of waiting and withdraw application.
5. Stall - branch officer irritates me.
6. Contemplate.
7. Approve -tomorrow.
8. Postpone - indefinitely.

No question. A man of action; pending.

TRAINING DIRECTOR

'I enjoy my work,' says Pearl Owens. 'Being the training director, is the most important job at the bank.'

What makes you think so?' I ask.

'Because,' she replies,'Money alone will not keep a bank alive. People do; and they must be people who know what they are doing.'

'Then why aren't you one of the best paid people on staff? Doesn't anyone realize the value of your contribution?'

'Maybe. Top management knows. But they pay only what they have to. No one really stops to figure out what the end result of my work is worth to this bank.'

'That's nuts! I exclaim. 'Why do you stay?'

Pearl shrugs her shoulders and says, 'I been meaning to look for another job, but I somehow never get around to it.'

She is such a warm, sympathetic, understanding woman that she tolerates injustice from high places. She will make suggestions but will not attempt to force her ideas on others.

She exudes confidence; inspires trainees to do their very best. They develop longstanding 'mother counselor' relationships with her. They love her - all 180 pounds of her.

Pearl has been meaning to do something about her weight. Maybe a new kind of diet. She's waiting until next Monday to start — that will be the sixth start this year — since September.

Now she's thinking it would be better to wait until after the Holidays are over. Why not wait for more favorable conditions?

Speaking of waiting, you are lucky you are not in Pearl's car pool. She has a perfect record. Never on time.

Always late when she drives. Never ready when someone else drives.

Can she tell time? Yes.

But she's got a lot of her to move. One extra English muffin; one more cup of hot coffee; one more five minutes in the shower;one more glance at T.V.; one more this or that and she's running behind schedule.

For Pearl, the above come as a package deal - invariable preceded by an alarm clock thrice silenced.

Marie arrived at Pearl's house five minutes early last Thursday morning. A very bad mistake.

'Jeez, Pearl,' she said, 'you just crawled outa bed. From the looks of you it'll take a month before you're ready. We ain't waitin. See you tomorrow.'

They drove off.

'A month!' said Pearl. 'I'll kill her.'

But she won't.

It only becomes one more thing she will never get around to doing.

THE PRESIDENT HIMSELF

I would be remiss indeed if I failed to have you meet the bank president — himself.

He is an ardent fisherman. He never tells fish stories. Pictures speak louder than words.

He looks rich.

Hudson Osmond Grimes is tall, stately, gracious, and cultured.

He is rich — very rich.

Yet, he is friendly, gregarious and beloved throughout the area. He prefers to deal with people in a favorable, social environment.

He is very democratic; and believes in voting — voting based on the number of shares you own.

Hudson is very civic minded. As a past president of the local Rotary Club, he can proudly point to the many beautification projects initiated during his term.

One day he phoned Mayor Thomas Doosby and asked, 'Tom, do you think this would be a good year to clean up and beautify the city park along the riverside?'

'I agree with you, ' answered the mayor, 'except the city council is unwilling to authorize funds. It would cost taxpayers a lot of money.'

'It was one of your campaign promises.'

'Yes,' agreed the mayor, 'Except certain contingencies have arisen which were not foreseeable at the time.'

'Tom. This is Hudson calling.'

Well, I ah— ah. My secretary didn't say who was calling. I should have recognized your voice. Poor connection.

'You know how it is Hud, can't let every Tom, Dick, and Harry know what I'm up to before we break the news in the press.'

'I understand how it is Mayor. Would you like me to send the bank's PR man over to help your people prepare a publicity release? He's good at it you know.'

'That's great Hud. Do you suppose you could find time to be in the picture with me when we break the story?'

Publicity and popularity have a way of going together. Hudson Grimes is very, very popular.

Social awareness and broad recognition for good deeds in the community is important to any bank - especially to a friendly bank.

Hudson is currently president of Mercy Hospital Board of Directors; past president of Hopkins Free Library; lifetime chairman of the Osmond Arts Museum; a member of the Board of Deacons of the Presbyterian Church; a director of United Fund; and also of the local Red Cross Chapter.

In addition to this, he serves on the United Council of Churches; the Hope House committee; the Saratoga Performing Arts Council; the Veterans Of Foreign Wars local chapter; the local Board of Education; the Capital District Council of Boy Scouts of America; and a few others I forgot to write down.

He is past president of the prestigious Lake George Club. It is only an hour and a half up the Northway and within minutes he can be sailing the beautiful waters of the Queen of American Lakes.

At the Winding Brook Country Club, he is past president, board member, and a four handicap golfer. Old cronies there call him 'Ozzy'.

Did his original wealth come from the Osmond family and the Poduck Iron Ore Mines?

I think so.

What a fortune. Dug right out of the beautiful Adirondacks before the turn of the century.

No wonder that the governor made him a member of the Adirondack Park Agency.

The obit editor of the Gazette has a note posted on the corner of his desk which says, 'Whenever Hudson Osmond Grimes dies give him a full page spread.'

With this extensive network of active contacts, plus the power and prestige of the bank, Hud finds it easy to influence whatever suits him at the time.

He does not misuse his power. He is good to the people at the bank; gives them free coffee; a lovely recreation-lunch room in most branches; a mid-winter party; and a summer cook-out at Hidden Valley Dude Ranch; a profit sharing plan; a bank stock purchase plan; a pension plan; blue cross protection; and other suitable fringe benefits.

Salaries are competitive.

He earns, but does not need his own $179,000 a year salary, plus profit sharing, plus a new cadillac each year, plus Board fees, plus six weeks vacation, plus a liberal expense account, and a few special perks that go with the office of Chairman of the Board, Chief Executive Officer, and Bank President.

At a Board meeting he said, 'Gentlemen, I would be willing to work for $1.00 a year and forego all the perks.'

'Mr. Chairman,' interrupted attorney Benson, 'I beg to differ. You are indeed most gracious. However, such action would be inappropriate, demeaning to the titles you hold, and precedent setting. The position you hold demands that proper compensation be granted.'

'Well — I ah,' Hud said.

And that was it.

He knew how to accept defeat.

Would you ever suspect that a man of such great and widespread involvement would procrastinate — on anything?

When would he ever find time to do so?

I guess you don't really know Hud. He is very resourceful.

Only last week, on four consecutive days, his secretary, Betty, placed seven calls; and each time said, 'I'm calling for Mr. Grimes. He planned to, but will not be able to attend today's meeting. Something unexpected came up.'

That was true too.

No one had expected the salmon trout to be biting like crazy in Lake George this late in the season.

Putting off attending a meeting is one thing. Neglecting nature is another.

A proposal has been presented to him at the bank. It says, 'In order to maintain our competitive advantage, we consider it imperative that this bank install automatic teller machines in all our branches.'

The proposal is complete. It justifies the cost and the advantages of providing the public with 24-hour banking service.

Hud is contemplating testing one of the machines personally before presenting it to the full Board.

He has been contemplating for three weeks — or maybe more.

Twice he has driven to Albany to personally observe one of the machines in operation during off hours at a branch of National Commercial Bank and Trust.

Much smarter to see it being operated by a customer than by a salesman.

The first customer, a sharp young man - probably a computer type - approaches the machine with confidence; inserts a card; waits several seconds and then the machine disgorges a packet of money. The young man doesn't even count it. He stuffs it in his pocket and drives off.

The next customer is a pleasant lady in her mid-forties. She takes out her card and moves toward the machine; hesitates, reads her card; then reads directions on the face of the machine. She is still uncertain and starts to leave.

Then she notices Hud nearby and says, 'Pardon me sir, but could you show me how to use this darn machine?'

Sorry, young lady. I have an anti-gadget phobia; I never buy anything from a machine. That's not banking, anyway.'

'You're right,' she replied. 'Damn banks.'

One more customer approaches the teller machine. He appears prosperous, tired and unsteady. A breathalizer could tell you why. Four times he tries to insert his card.

'Hold still,' he says.

On the fifth pass the slot holds still and his card goes in. No money comes out. Neither does his card 'Bastard,' he says. 'Gimme my money. Gimme back my card.'

The mechanical monster ignores him.

He pounds it in the face; kicks it in the shins; and hammers it in the chest. No money. No card.

Infuriated, the customer jumps in his car; burns rubber in search of a DWI.

By now, Hud is convinced. His survey proves that 'two out of three customers have problems with the machine.'

He will further postpone any action on the proposal; and he does.

A voice inside of Hud keeps saying, 'It ain't natural to do business with a machine. Too damned impersonal. 'Better wait; someday they'll accept the monsters.'

See how important a procrastinator of Hud's stature can be to progress. He keeps it from rushing forward and plunging headlong into the sea like lemmings.

Hudson Osmond Grimes is making one more important contribution to society which may speed his entry into the ranks of SuperPRO.

He is writing a book.

Or at least, he is intending to write a book. He has already made thirty or forty important notations - within the past year and a half.

The subject is important. He owes it to historians and the good citizens of the area to enlighten them on their heritage.

Although specific, the modest title is appropriate: 'Grimes Contribution To Our Capitol District Heritage.'

Rating Hud's standing in SuperPRO ranks may become difficult.

There is a fine line between legitimate procrastination and being physically unable to attend an excessive number of overlapping meetings.

Hudson O. Grimes is forever crossing back and forth across that line.

There are others within the hierarchy of the bank who rate attention as possible candidates for SuperPRO, but we don't have time to meet all of them.

Furthermore, we do not want to overlook the worthiness of some representative staff members. These are the people who are called 'bank employees', which means they are the ones who cannot park in the spaces reserved for bank officers.

The bank does not foster a cast system. Heavens no. Everybody is on the same payroll. They have separate johns.

Is there anyone special you would like to meet from the employee group? That attractive blonde teller?

Okay. She's a good one.

Her name is Sylvia Ann Duncan. She is the self-anointed sex symbol of Upstate National and all its branches.

If she had not anointed herself, she certainly would have won the designation in any unbiased election.

She is stacked; vivacious; energetic; enthusiastic; enthralling; and a compulsive gossip.

Men are attracted to her - not because of her gossip. However, a lot of women love her too.

She is the 'thrill of the month' for old codgers.

Do you know what a bank lobby looks like on April 3, or any other 3rd of the month?

The lineup in front of her teller window resembles a Veteran's Day Parade; proud old soldiers standing tall, smiling. Shuffling spritely every time the line of march moves forward.

'Boy, am I glad to see you,' says Sylvia as each man reaches her window. 'You look so good today. Here, use my pen to endorse you Social Security check.'

If that meant touching her hand — for ever so brief a moment — what harm could it do?

It certainly can't hurt Sylvia. She is only twenty nine. She has been a teller at the bank since she turned seventeen.

Sylvia is sensitive to people's feelings. On the 3rd of the month, she refuses to take her mandatory half-hour lunch break.

This infuriates Ms Titsworth, who says 'This is gross insubordination. We will have to terminate her.'

'Overruled,' replies President Grimes.

Which, of course, gives Ms Titsworth ample incentive to build a documentary file of ever increasing proportions for Sylvia — or perhaps against Sylvia.

Heretofore, undetected by Ms Titsworth, Sylvia has always postponed doing the many important little things that contribute to the efficiency and greater productivity of a bank teller. Sylvia very well knows all of the things she is supposed to do.

'Someday,' says Sylvia, 'I am going to reorganize my teller drawers. They'll be so neat, no one will believe it.'

They won't either.

Because Sylvia has become an inveterate procrastinator.

Every day, the head teller has to wait for Sylvia's shipping money (her surplus cash). Each day Sylvia promises, 'I'll have it ready early tomorrow.'

It never is.

During rush hours, Sylvia often hurries to the head teller's cage saying, 'Marie I need more fives. I planned on getting them earlier but I got too busy.'

'You're never too busy to gossip though, are you?'

Sylvia knows Marie is jealous because so many customers prefer to come to her window.

On the other hand, Sylvia is envious of Marie and several other tellers whose names appear almost monthly in the bank's Upstate Weekly. The column is headed Tellers Without Errors ' and lists those who have not had a cash difference during any of the past three consecutive months.

It is not all that easy to accomplish.

Concentration is the key to it.

Any teller can count to ten - or even to one hundred. Maybe you can too?

But can you do it without breaking your concentration? Not just once a day. But hundreds of times, even thousands of times, day after day, week after week.

The only way a teller can make a mistake is to break their concentration - or let it be broken by someone else.

Starting tomorrow, Sylvia will concentrate.

No more gossip.

Promise.

TAKE A BREAK

Have you seen enough representatives of the world of banking to convince yourself that procrastinators are abiding therein?

Okay.

Then let's take a break.

Suppose we try sitting in on at least part of a Wednesday night meeting of the Adirondack Pasteboard Association.

There are eight men present. Each man is, or was, at least President, CEO, Senior Vice President, or Board Chairman of some successful business organization.

Each is accustomed to making important decisions. In these weekly meetings, each man is called upon to make many fast and important decisions; on his own; no help from anone. If he makes a wrong decison. It can be costly — and often is.

Charlie Green is new to the group. If he shows he is capable of devoting himself solely to the business at hand, he will become a regular member of the group. He must also be willing and able to contribute financially — when it becomes necessary.

Jim Abbott sponsored and introduced Charlie to the group. Jim did not know why Charlie had recently retired, at age forty-eight from the insurance business. It does not matter, anyway. There is no time to make irrelevant explanations at these meetings.

What does matter is that Jim evidently put off telling Charlie about the group's unwritten rules. Jim, himself, is still not very good at observing the code of silence.

It may soon cost him his membership.

Jim should know by now that the group has absolutely no interest whatsoever — on any Wednesday evening —

in anything but the fulfillment of their individual objectives.

Anything which distracts can be costly.

Jim has been playing too much bridge with his wife. He can chatter all he wants to when playing bridge. It is even polite to do so — especially if you have a tidbit of local gossip.

But not here.

So it is Jim's fault that Charlie got himself trapped in extraneous conversation.

Jim asks 'What makes you look so tired tonight, Charlie?'   'I been busy.'

'Doing what ? You're retired.'

'Around the house, Jim — around the house.'

'Doing what?'

'I was waiting for the new kid to show up to mow the lawn.'

'Hell, you could mow it yourself.'

'I was meaning to. But I got to thinking, a kid could use the money.'

'What happened to the first kid?'

'He charged ten bucks and it took him an hour and a half to mow it. I stood there and watched him.'

'What did this kid charge?'

'Twelve bucks. But he's better — lots better. He did it all in an hour — saved me a lotta time.'

By now, I hope you truly understand and appreciate the rationale of that last statement. A dedicated procrastinator does not like to have other people waste his time.

He reserves that privilege for himself.

By the same token, the President of the Adirondack Pasteboard Association reserves the right to keep its members in line. So he says, 'Look, you guys. You know the rules. Save your stories for the coffee break.'

'It's my fault,' Abbott confessed. 'I guess I never got around to telling Charlie about that rule.'

'I'm just as bad,' says Charlie, 'I never got around to asking.'

'Well you know now,' replies the Pres. and hands Charlie fifty-two red pasteboards.

'Deal,' he says.

'Okay, men. Five card stud. Open on any pair. Bet or get out — up to twenty five.'

ATTORNEY-AT-LAW

Now, let's shift our attention to some other area of the business world.

Would it be fair to take an 'insider's look at an attorney's office?

Why not?

Bear in mind that this research was in one individual office only. It is in no way to be construed as being representative of typical legal offices or any other legal office in the land. Just one isolated case that my research assistant was able to uncover.

Sometimes a researcher gets lucky.

I consider this body of research so important that I have instructed her to file full documentation with the President of Procrastinators Club of North America.

It is important to start preserving all meaningful information about SuperPROS for the enlightenment of future generations. No one has previously gotten around to it.

Much of our culture heritage can be reflected by what we see in the luxurious office of Bullet, Abrahams, and DiBiano Attornies at Law.

It is strategically located downtown near city hall and the county courthouse in a midsize American city. Samuel O. Bullet, the founder and original member of the now prestigious law firm, had selected the site in the early days.

A cantankerous contemporary once said , 'The only reason Sam picked that site was because he never got to court on time. Being next door was supposed to make him on time. But it never did.'

A next generation observer added, 'The same is true of his grandson, Peter. Do you suppose that procrastination is an inherited trait?'

Not everyone is blessed with such a heritage. It gives an unfair advantage.

Far too many people have not traced their roots and therefore cannot rely on early traces of procrastination. You may be only a budding genius who has not yet proved himself. Far better that you develop the craft yourself and not depend on uncertain bloodlines.

Let's not dilly dally any longer. Time we got inside that law office to observe first hand how cleverly these legal eagles apply the principles of procrastination.

The first person we see is grandson Peter Bullet.

It is 10:55 A.M.. He is just arriving for work. Why is he late this morning? Who knows? He is always late.

He hurries up the steps; bursts through the outer office door and says, 'Sorry I'm late. Was unavoidably delayed at the courthouse.'

Not so.

But an astute attorney is expected to not only defend his clients but himself as well. It is too bad that Peter employed such questionable veracity. Almost always one finds that an attorney tells the truth, the whole truth, and nothing but the truth.

Isn't that your experience?

That's good.

Because, as I have already told you, Peter Cunningham Bullet is not atypical of those who practice in this honored and revered profession.

You will be able to judge that for yourself after spending at least part of a day in his exhalted presence.

MAKE A GOOD IMPRESSION

Attorney Bullet knew full well the importance of giving his clients a visible impression of the expediency with which each case is being handled.

'Make it appear as if you are doing all you possibly can, as fast as you can,' were the instructions he remembered so well from Grandfather S. O. Bullet.

This, as you can see, is a very important piece of advice to be kept in mind by anyone espousing to become a respected member of the procrastinators' inner circle.

His very first move, after dispensing with the niceties of the day with his client reinforced his dedication to this creed.

He pressed the button on his intercom and said, 'Miss Collins, please get me the law firm of McNairy, McGillicudy, and Kohn. I want to speak with Andrews.'

He turned and said, 'Mrs. Tuttle, I can't understand why your husband failed to engage one of the principals of the firm. We would not be facing all these delays if more experienced counsel were representing him.'

'Why do you think I am divorcing him? That's the way Robert does everything.'

When the phone buzzed, he picked it up and immediately complained, 'Andrews you know how anxious I am to get some speedy action from your client, Robert A. Tuttle. What in sin's name is holding it up. Can't you get him to agree to my client's reasonable requests for a very fair and equitable settlement in this divorce action?'

'You horse's ass. I just found those papers from you in this morning's mail. Is the old broad sitting at your desk and you're trying to make a big impression?'

'Yes that's the case, Andrews. We want action. And we want it soon or we're going to make additional demands.'

'Good. That'll run up your fees. And mine too. I'll stall this reply another two weeks. Is our golf date still on for 2:30 this afternoon?'

'Yes it is. You know how trying and humiliating a divorce action can be. Why can't you get Tuttle to get this over with as soon as possible? We don't want any counter demands. We just want action. So move it will you?'

'Pete, they don't call you P.C.B. for nothing. Your delaying tactics make it almost impossible to dispose of any case.'

'How's that?'

'The Tuttles were ready for a quick, uncontested divorce. But you never got the paper work to me. Now they're both hot, mad, and ready to stick it to each other as much as the law will allow. PCB, I love you.'

'The feeling is mutual. I warn you. My client is going to seek greater compensation if you don't get action by this time next week.'

With that, Attorney Bullet slammed down the phone; turned to his client and said, 'Sorry for my burst of anger, Mrs. Tuttle. But I just can't tolerate these people who don't get things done when they're supposed to.'

'I think you did the right thing, and, Mr. Bullet, if Robert procrastinates any more, I certainly will demand all I am entitled to.'

Obviously impressed that her attorney was doing all he could on her behalf. She left the law office wondering why she had ever agreed with Robert to a quick and amicable settlement, in the first place.

Peter Bullet leaned back in his swivel chair and said to himself,

'It never ceases to amaze me how these unavoidable delays become so very, very productive.'

SELF-FORGIVENESS

Having been privileged to witness Peter Bullet in action, I hope you have realized the importance of forgiving yourself for any measure of procrastination on your part.

Why blame yourself?

Why develop a feeling of guilt?

After all, if Peter Bullet had acted promptly on behalf of his client, he would have deprived her of the satisfaction of punishing her estranged husband. She would also have forsaken the possibility of a more generous settlement.

An established procrastinator learns to keep things in perspective. Which is what we should do.

At his prices, we can't afford to spend an entire day with a SuperPRO like Peter Bullet. We will return at some future date when we can afford him.

Is that okay by you?

WHAT ABOUT TAXES?

Our researcher, who discovered the library incident, is very good.

For the past several months, she has been devoting most of her time to 'taxes'. If she ever gets around to turning in her full report, I will share it with you. In the mean time, we can overview some of her incomplete early observations.

She says, 'You won't believe how many people procrastinate about their taxes. The figures are absolutely mind-boggling. Almost everybody does — in one way or another.'

116

She may be right. But like so many other poll takers. She has not been able to contact all taxpayers. Conclusions, based on samplings, are subject to wide variations of error. Be thankful you are not a major politician, or a national television program director.

You could make our survey more complete if you will send a brief note telling us how you handle your taxes.

Do you postpone any of your tax record keeping? Do you delay filing your tax form until the last day?

That is the sort of information that will help make Evelyn's report more valid.

You could also urge your friends to get a copy of this book and send us a similar note to make our survey even more complete.

Evelyn says, 'I am appalled at the number of people who put off keeping simple tax records throughout the year.'

'What good would it do?'

'A lot,' she replies.'Records can save people more tax money than they think.'

But it's complicated — isn't it?'

'No it is not. It's simple — easy, and worth the time and effort. Just stash every pertinent receipt and cancelled check in an envelope each month: or toss them in an old shoe box until tax time.'

'A friend of mine did that one year. But it didn't do him any good.'

'Why not?'

'He didn't have time to sort them over and put them into proper categories.'

'How come?'

'Well — he put off doing his taxes until late evening — and he had to rush.'

'Why?'

It was Monday, April 15th.'

Evelyn shakes her head and says, 'It's unbelievable the number of people who delay filing their taxes until the last week — the last day — or the last hour — or right up to the last minute.'

I wonder — should I tell her I'm one of them, and thus improve the accuracy of her survey?

Evelyn says, 'My cousin, Mildred, is a good example of people who put off doing their taxes to the last minute.

'Mildred resolved to file her 1983 tax form no later than January 10, 1984. But come the 10th, she discovers she has not yet received her W-2 form from her boss. He tells her to be patient — the girl in the office meant to have them out early but has been delayed.

'So Mildred waits and waits. Twice more she asks the boss. More delay. But she finally gets the W-2 on February 9.

'By now Mildred's resolve is less than luke warm. How can she possibly think about doing taxes right now? She's got a date to go skiing for the weekend in Vermont.

'Mildred's luke warm turns to hot — not for taxes — but for the ski instructor.'

'Why should that delay her tax filing?' I ask.

'Because Mildred's got a torrid affair going. No way is she going to waste time on something she can put off. She's got' til April 15 to file the damn thing anyway.'

'But I thought you told me Mildred wanted to get an early refund?'

'That's true,'replies Evelyn. 'And a coupla times, Mildred gets the forms out. But each time she decided to wait until she is better prepared with all her figures.'

I take it, that never happens.'

'You're right,' says Evelyn, 'not until the evening of April 15. Even then, Mildred is determined to file the long form and take advantage of all she is entitled to.'

'Does she?' I ask.

'She tries,' replies Evelyn. 'She's got stuff spread out all over the kitchen table. Checkbook, cancelled checks, bank mortgage statement, paid bills, guidebook by Lasser, another by Block, and IRS Publication 17 — the whole bit.'

'Are her taxes that complicated?' I ask.

'Not really. Mildred just makes a big deal out of them. That's probably why she procrastinates. She thinks its going to be such a horrendous job.'

'Does it help her to have all those guidebooks?'

'No. Any one of them will do. By waiting until the last day, she goes wild trying to locate info anyway — and ends up basically copying last year's form — and not getting the full benefit of tax breaks.'

Looks to me as if Mildred is a prime candidate for SuperPRO — providing she has learned how to postpone lots of other things too. IRS must love her, me, and millions of others like us. No one knows how many millions of dollars in extra revenue we procrastinators contribute to the government.

What a superbly patriotic thing to do.

On the other hand, Evelyn's research has turned up some procrastinators who are not in good favor with the IRS. These are the people who wait until the last minute can't figure out what to do — don't hire someone to do their taxes for them — are not on anybody's reported payroll — and delay filing a tax report — ever.

Fear, foolishness, or forgetfulness will win you no points with IRS. Don't delay beyond the point of no return.

If you want to pick up SuperPRO points on late taxes, do it on local property taxes. First you get slapped with late penalty fees, reminders — then a legal notice of tax sale. Your property gets sold. No more property taxes for you. Hurrah!

And you do not go to jail.

HOME REPAIRS

There is another, more subtle method, for a dedicated procrastinator to lose a house, but not the taxes that go with it.

Our researchers find, however, that very few people have the tenacity to stick with this method until All is lost. Reducing the value of the house is relatively easy.

But to go to absolute zero takes far more years than most individuals can sustain. The reasons are many and complex; and are most often the result of peer pressure.

Let's visit Fred Degan and see how he applies this method.

Fred is a truck driver for one of the major construction firms in the area. He is also known as a 'handyman'. He is smart. If anything is broken, Fred can figure out how to fix it. He is forever helping neighbors, friends, and relatives with their 'fix-it' problems.

But what happens at Fred's own house?

You guessed it. Nothing.

For instance, just last week his wife, Alma says, 'Fred, that bedroom window is sticking agian. When are you gonna fix it?'

'Just as soon as I can get to it, Babe. It can wait a coupla days.'

'That's what you said about a lotta other things,' she complains. 'The kitchen screen door — the rotted rail on the back porch—the cellar light switch — the drippy faucet in the bathroom — the busted hinge on the bedroom door — the jammed drawer in the kitchen cabinet — and . . . '

Fred interrupted, 'Those are all little things, Babe. I'll get them all done as soon as I can.'

'You want big? How about painting the house?'

'It's been raining too much lately. I been waiting for it to dry out.'

'Dry out! Fred, you've been waiting over six years for it to dry out. It's so dry and flaky now, it looks like a bowl of cornflakes.'

'I know. But I gotta do the roof first. It's beginning to leak a little.'

'A little! You apple head. When it's raining I can't even cook. I got every damn pot and pan catching dripping water in every room upstairs. I'm a one-woman bucket brigade racing to dump water in the bathtub, which incidently also has a broken shower head.'

'You're right, Alma. See how important it is for me to put off those other things until I get that roof fixed. I even noticed the ceiling in the spare bedroom sagging. Must be water trapped overhead somehow.'

'Not anymore, Buster. The whole damn thing busted this morning and fell on top of the bed. Now we got our own original — an inside-out waterbed.'

121

'I better take a look.'

'No need to track that mess all over the house. Just go in Teddy's room. You can look thru the hole he kicked in the wall when he was four years old. Remember how you postponed patching it 'til he got a little bigger.'

'Yeah, I wanted to wait 'til he grew outa that kid stuff.'

'Fred, your son graduates from college next month.'

'Maybe I can get Teddy to give me a hand fixing the old place up this summer.'

'Why bother? It ain't worth a plug nickel anymore.'

'It sure is. They ain't reduced the tax assessment on it none.'

'Who ever heard of them reducing an assessment?'

'It's worth more than you think. Soon as I find time, I'll get it fixed up like it was new. Just you wait and see.'

'I'm waiting Freddy, boy. I'm waiting.'

Such constant nagging and implied lack of confidence can be very debilitating to anyone who is seeking SuperPRO status. Only the

staunchest of procrastinators can resist caving in — and making all of those home repairs exactly as he had intended to in the first place.

OUR PRO BASED ECONOMY

Procrastinators are the great unsung heroes of our economy. I mentioned earlier in this book that to suddenly eliminate procrastinators from our society would create an economic disaster, panic, and financial chaos —the likes of which we have never seen before.

That's true.

And confidentially attested to at a recent clandestine meeting at our mountainside headquarters.

Would you believe that we had a devil of a time setting up this meeting?

Why?

Because we developed a proposed agenda and asked a variety of business people to be prepared to tell how dependent they were on procrastinators for business. Nobody wanted to talk about it publicly — even in a closed meeting.

So my chief researcher says, 'To Hell with it. Just let's invite a bunch of them over for a weekend blast — beer, hot dogs, hamburgers, steaks, fried chicken, swimming, boating — fun and frolic — whatever they want to do.'

What a turnout. Way beyond our fondest dreams.

Just to give you an idea, I'll name a few. They represent a broad cross-section of our economy. You may know some of them and realize that they are not listed in the order of their importance.

Here's the partial list:

richman, poorman
merchant, chief
beggarman, thief
doctor, lawyer
banker, sawyer
tinker, tailor
cowboy, sailor

dentist, priest
policeman, preacher
inn keeper, jeweler

surgeon
repairman
psychiatrist
technician
salesman
singer
druggist
broker
beautician

To bring such a polyglot together takes a rustic environment — like a melting pot of Early America — the right circumstances — good food, fine beverages, — an eager and alert research team — gentle persuasion; and no announced purpose.

Yet after about an hour, our purpose began to take shape when a beeper signaled Dr. Sullivan to call his office. He did, and a few of us could hear him say, 'Dammit, if Jack hadn't put off getting his annual check up, he wouldn't be facing this emergency. Get him prepped for O.R. I'll be there in fifteen minutes.'

As Dr. Sullivan excused himself and drove off, Warren Wilson said,'The last time Jack refilled his prescription, I told him he better get in to see Doc. A little of the right medicine would have fixed him up for a few bucks. Now emergency surgery is going to cost him a bundle.

Tough on Jack, but good for the ambulance crew, emergency room staff, extra nurses, hospital income, linen and laundry service — and a lot of others — including me. More prescriptions and get well cards. And his wife will get all worked up and need more sleeping pills, aspirin, and chocolate candy.'

'You make it sound so crass,' said Father O'Neil. 'You in the field of medicine are there to help people.'

'Right Father. We heal bodies. You heal souls. Let's face it Father, it's a business and people who postpone proper care create more work and income for everyone.'

'Are you saying, people would lose jobs if it weren't for procrastinators?'

'Sure. Might even affect the clergy.'

'How's that?'

'People who can't seem to find time to stop their sinning -or follow the teachings of the Lord are the ones who need the most help from you.'

'Those same characters keep us on the go,' said Police Chief Brian McCarthy, as he joined the conversation. 'As long as those guys put off going straight, we need a lotta cops.'

'That's true,' said Judge Wyman Bean. 'Without the criminal element, where would all the lawyers, court clerks, bail bondsmen and judges be?'

'Don't forget prison wardens, guards, clerks,inspectors, legislators, counselors, and tons of others who are part of our corrections and rehabilitation system,' said Warden Max Robinson.

'Wait a minute. remember, there's two sides to every coin,' said Karl Clearwater. 'Who do you think provides the opportunities for us? As a former master jewel thief, I say it's those who delay installing proper locks on doors and windows — who invite us to steal.'

'For you, Karl,' said Judge Bean, 'any wealthy person who postpones installing the most sophisticated security equipment is asking for it.'

'Thank you, Your Honor.'

'Which reminds me,' interrupted Samuel Polinsky of the IRS. 'I've been meaning to thank you Karl. Your episodes led us to several people who couldn't produce evidence to substantiate their considerable wealth.' 'You mean the ones who never got around to reporting income?'

'That's right. Those people give a lot of work to our field investigating staff. Then when they get caught, they scramble like hell to hire a good tax accountant and a tax lawyer.'

'Instead of praise, could you reward me with tax forgiveness? You know damn well I never realized any income on that last job. The cops caught me red-handed and impounded it all — and I'm still paying taxes on it.'

'Sorry, old man. Read the law.'

'How can IRS do that?' Asked garage owner Neil Tripp.

'Income is income,' replied Polinsky. 'Stolen income spends faster, that's all.'

'Man — and my customers accuse me of being a bandit on repair jobs. They can't escape you. But they could put me completely outa business if they did what they should, when they should.'

'Like what?'

'Like coming to see me when they first think something's wrong with their car. But no. They put it off until it's convenient or until they bust down on the road and get soaked for a tow job.

'Or they dilly dally and don't check the oil, the battery, the plugs, the fan belt. The radiator — the little things. Next they postpone getting a tune up — and I end up with the big bucks in a nice juicy overhaul job. Suits me. I need the dough.'

'You need the dough,' exclaimed Saul O. Ginsburg. 'What about a merchant like me? I got inventory, I got overhead, I got high rent, I got clerks who stand around half the day doing nothing.'

'I got display counters loaded with merchandise. But do shoppers buy? No. They wander around my store, using up my heat, my lights, my carpeting, my patience — putting off buying — until some other time. I hate procrastinators.'

'You love 'em, Saul,' said Nate Kohn.

'Why should I?'

'Because from them you get your biggest profits — especially at Christmas time.'

'How so?'

'Because they are the ones who rush into your store at the last minute' desperate to buy anything in sight. They clean out all your junk at top prices. Two weeks later, you get rid of the same stuff at 60% discount — and still make a profit.'

'Well, maybe — a little. So I should love procrastinators   except they should wait so long my ulcers work overtime waiting for them to buy. Oiey!'

What a fertile ground for me and my research assistants. We kept tuning in on a wide variety of conversations — which we later fed into our computers.

Conclusions based on analysis of information thus obtained; and upon follow-up interviews proves beyond a shadow of doubt that the total impact of countless procrastinators becomes a dynamic force within our economy.

So dynamic, in fact, that it permeates every level of economic activity at town, city, county, state, national and international level.

It's effect is by no means restricted to our Adirondack Region and the Great North East business centers, wherein most of our research was concentrated.

I would provide you with all the minute data if I had not discovered that 98.9% of you would put off reading the report until later, and later,and later — and on into eternity.

Some of you would want me to transfer it by modem into your home computers so you could review it fully at a more favorable time. If you want to absorb all the costs involved (including research time) I would be willing to take it under advisement.

However, as John Dean would say, 'At this point in time', it is more important to provide you with a broad understanding of the contribution of procrastinators to our economy — and leave the details to qualified statisticians.

For instance, is it necessary to know precisely how many people are employed as garage mechanics to recognize that they are important to our economy? Try to find one when your car breaks down.

Even if we knew the number of mechanics, how could we tell how many are employed because of procrastinators? We need only do what Economists do — extrapolate.

But, for goodness sake, if we do that, let's do it in English. Economists speak a foreign language — so foreign that it is not recognizable in English , French, German, Spanish, Japanese, Russian or Pig Latin.

Better we should do like Phil Donohue or Johnny Carson — deal with the meat of the subject. Everybody understands them — (except maybe a wife or two)

As with the need for garage mechanics, we can understand the need for other kinds of repairmen, too — much of that need being generated by procrastinators.

Their numbers would be nowhere near as great if it were not for neglect — which is just another way of saying procrastination.

Certainly no one pays good money for a useful piece of equipment and then says, 'I am going to deliberately neglect my new lawn mower, bicycle, roto tiller, boat, vacuum cleaner, swimming pool, lawn furniture, golf clubs, typewriter, and pet rock.'

A STITCH

IN TIME

No sir. The intention is to always keep it properly oiled, painted, cleaned, covered and protected from the weather, or whatever else is necessary to keep it running or looking good.

But within a short time you fail to take proper care of it. Your neglect hastens breakdowns, rust, and useability - to the point where you must take it to someone more knowledgeable in restoring its usefulness.

REPAIRS

That means employment not only for the person who repairs the item but for those who supply the replacement of prematurely wornout parts.

And, of course, the repairmen need someone to supply them with tools, a business site, heat, lights, telephone service, etc., etc., ' in a domino chain of inter-related business transactions.

In a recent broadcast, Paul Harvey said '70% of all jobs are service jobs - performing some service, rather than manufacturing something.'

He didn't explain who generates the need for so much service. Is it because so many people put off doing things for themselves? Does it apply just to Chicago, the state of Illinois, or to the entire United States?

As soon as I get a chance, I'll call him and ask.

In the meantime, we are co-operating with those who wish to form local chapters of Procrastinators Club of North America. It causes postponements on lots of other things we should be doing, but first things first.

How can we overlook serving the needs of kindred procrastinators for comradeship and unity?

I hope you don't think I am digressing from 'our economy' when talking about the need for and existence of clubs in the USA.

I am not.

The number of people enrolled in major clubs alone is almost unbelievable. Our research shows the following:

Rotary	909,750
Kiwanis	304,021
Lions	1,350,711
Masonic	1,767,914
Knights of Columbus	1,349,724
Zonta	32,000
Links	5,200
DAR	208,000
Eagles	695,500
Elks	1,650,002
Grange	425,000
Jaycees	300,000
Hibernians	191,000
American Legion	2,600,000
Total	11,784,088

That's an impressive figure — and does not include hundreds of smaller clubs of local or national importance.

What impact do they have on our economy?

Add up the weekly or monthly meals, hotel rooms at conventions, miles traveled, paid speakers, specialized magazines and other literature, uniforms, pins, plaques, rings and other jewelry.

And a wee bit o' booze.

People who belong to these clubs have a worthy purpose in mind when they join — most often a business related one such as 'I can make a lot of new friends who are sure to remember me when they need something in my line.'

And naturally, everyone is primarily concerned with 'being of service' to people in the community.

Some—possibly procrastinators are accused of using club responsibilities as an excuse for getting out of less interesting work at the office — at home — at the mill — at the factory — or at the store.

Even if this could be proven, we could not afford to disband the clubs. How could our economy function without this incidental patronizing.

FUNERAL DIRECTORS

The most exemplary members of clubs are often funeral directors. Why? Because they seldom belong to just one club — but to as many as possible. They are active, friendly and duly concerned about the welfare of their fellow beings — and to maintain high visibility in the community. Perhaps the end justifies the means.

When under the influence, one director said, 'We are not very fond of procrastinators — those who put off the inevitable beyond a reasonable time.'

'Why?'

'Because at the peak of your career, a family will show proper respect and provide you with a suitable funeral. When you are ancient and almost forgotten, all they are looking for is a division of assets. Don't procrastinate.

'Get it done early.'

You, of course, know that you do not have to adhere closely to all the advice you are given; especially when the advice is free.

Better that you should pay the going rate in whatever field of advice you are seeking. Your chances of it being sound are considerably better - but not guaranteed.

'Advice' is big, BIG business. People with a wide variety of credentials, degrees, and egos 'give advice' (for a price). They are called consultants, counselors, writers, columnists, therapists, preachers, priests, psychologists, psychotherapists, ministers, psychoanalysts, psychiatrists, astrologists, fortune tellers, doctors, brokers, tipsters, gurus, coaches...

My goodness, is there no end to the list?

The value of their advice is not always proportional to the fee. Most of those in traditional clergy give advice freely and with great empathy. And it is often valuable beyond compare.

At the other extreme are those whose fees are so excessive they reek of vulgarity along with the quality of their exhortations from sumptuous offices.

Big wind. No rain.

You could get better results talking to yourself.

Be that as it may, it is important to realize that 'advice giving' generates a tremendous cashflow. And procrastinators are the principal prospects for advisors.

Pros come in many sizes, shapes, colors and creeds. They excel in dilly-dally and saying, 'Let's hire a consultant to get us out of this mess.'

The consultant opens your eyes to what you know you should have been doing in the first place.

You ask him, 'What time is it?'

He borrows your watch and replies, 'The time is NOW.'

My what a revelation. You tell your Board of Directors, your officers, your staff - and with the super recharge, your organization takes on new life - goes into high gear, totally eliminating all delays.

For a time, your status as a SuperPRO is diminished. It's tough. But you learn to live with it — for awhile.

During this revival period, you turn to your banker and say, 'We are entering a period of expansion and rebuilding — please, kind sir, increase our credit line.'

He reviews your current operating statement, your balance sheet, and the number of points he can charge you above the prime rate. He says, 'With the outlook in your industry and the renewed vigor in your own operations, our Board is willing to take on the added risk — providing you maintain higher compensating balances and provide us with additional collateral.'

What could be more reasonable?

Now you are in the same position as your competitors. Because of so many back-orders, they are now playing catch-up under the same ground rules.

Sooner or later, you and everyone else must do business with the bank. Your banker says, 'Don't delay. Get your money now, while it's red hot.'

As a confirmed procrastinator, all you hear is the magic word — 'delay' — and you go for it.

Since the bank is the hub of ALL business activity, you set off a chain of events that forces other procrastinators to get off their duffs and supply you with the goods and services you need.

'Go-getters' are the ones who keep the business world humming — or so we've been told.

But what do you think now?

It's obviously 'come-from-behinders' who trigger everything.

Can't you see that?

Where would the big profits be in the stock market if it were not for friends like Bob Jones who spots a hot stock — but postpones buying until sure that a bull-market exists — and prices are up? Then he buys — giving profiteers a chance to reap rich rewards.

Within a day or so, the market turns down. He has an impulse to sell so as not to suffer a loss. But in a high priced letter from his stock advisor, he reads,'This is merely a technical correction in the market.'

Thus assured, he hesitates to sell. He waits and watches the price on his stock go down and down. He says, 'Why should I sell now and take such a big loss? I'll wait for more favorable conditions.'

Again, he hesitates. Two weeks later in another stock advisory letter he reads,'The DOW is now below 1100 with no perceivable bottom in sight.' He panics and sells, much to the delight of a shrewd bull who has been watching from the sidelines.

Bob says, 'Boy, never again.'

Two months later, his broker phones and says, 'Bob, you're stock is climbing like crazy again. Wanna get back in?'

He does.

How else could a SuperPRO keep the wheels of fortune turning?

TAX PROCRASTINATORS

Very few people realize it, but tardy tax payments are big business — and another important example of how procrastinators contribute to employment in our economy.

Who would think that some two million procrastinators owe the federal government an estimated $7.7 BILLION (dollars) in tardy tax payments for 1983 and previous years?

Well, it's true.

I doubt that any members of Procrastinators Club of North America are in that group. At least I hope not. How could we tolerate a member who is going out of his mind from the constant ringing of his home telephone?

You see, that repeated ringing of the telephone is what is now happening to tax delinquents. It's all part of a nationwide computer and telephone system developed for the Internal Revenue Service to expedite the collection of taxes from tax delinqents.

Tax delinquent? Wouldn't you rather be called a 'procrastinator'?

But no matter how named, the improved procedure is the final link in a system designed to hound those who are unreasonably behind in paying their taxes. It is operating from 21 IRS centers across the nation.

Each computer identifies taxpayers who have ignored three previous IRS notices, and then starts automatically dialing their home or business telephone — until the phone is answered. If the computer gets no answer, it automatically redials.

Just like a teenager, it never tires of clinging to the phone until the desired party is reached.

Once the procrastinator is reached, IRS officers may pay them a personal visit. In the meantime, computers monitor cases until tardy payments are caught up.

By the use of this computerized system, so much paper work can be eliminated that IRS expects to be able to hire about 300 more revenue officers — and still cut the average cost of collecting an account by nearly 47 per cent.

Some big banks are also utilizing other computers to improve collections on tardy loan payments.

My researchers were unable to get any accurate figures on the number of people who are late in making payments to banks, credit unions, stores, and finance companies. Nor would they reveal the amount of money paid in late charges and extra interest.

And a loan shark was of no help either. He said, 'What late payments?'

However, it's safe to conclude that without procrastinators our economy would suffer greatly — bill collectors without jobs — reduced income from penalty charges — and diminished use of telephone service and computers.

From the evidence we have gathered and presented, business leaders and economists should be willing to admit that our economy would be in a shambles it it were not for the continuing contribution of our vast army of procrastinators.

Right?

SuperPROS EVERYWHERE

OLD FAITHFUL

Before I forget about it, I better let you know about a case of procrastination that is befuddling experts and government officials at Yellowstone National Park.

It's Old Faithful — the dramatic geyser who deservedly earned her name by spouting a silvery cascade of steaming water high into the air 'every hour on the hour' — or within a few minutes thereof.

Each of her 120 to 170 feet displays last about four minutes sending up 10,000 gallons of water at a temperature of about 200 degrees. Real hot stuff.

There are other more dramatic geysers that spout 200 feet or more and flow for two or three hours. But the amazing thing about Old Faithful was her predictability — as if created to accomodate the time schedules of hurrying tourists — who could take their seats and be guaranteed of a spectacular show without prolonged waiting.

Her dependability has made her famous for over 100 years. Since being discovered in 1870, she has not wavered, winter, summer, spring or fall — until recently.

She has finally discovered the gentle art of procrastination — and refuses to spout forth until she gets around to it; and this is very disturbing to visitors who may have to wait an extra twenty or thirty minutes for natures' splendor.

I wonder if any of these impatient ones are the same people who wait in line overnight for tickets to 'The Grateful Dead'? Nah — they couldn't be.

THE CALVIN COOLIDGE NON-RACE

This race is not yet as famous as the Olympics — yet its potential for attracting procrastinators is terrific. Some of our members are already in training.

An elaborate race course has been constructed for this major event in Scottsboro, Arizona. It is thirty three feet long.

The winner of the race is the athlete who can move the entire distance showing the least amount of motion — yet never stopping.

They don't know who won last year's race. The time-keeper fell asleep.

It was named after Calvin Coolidge who wisely said, 'I do not choose to run.'

WRITING FOR PUBLICATION

Writing is a profession which seems to have an endless fascination for those best suited to become members of the SuperPRO Hallowed Hall of Hesitation.

I know a writer who writes very well — so well in fact that almost anything he writes is highly saleable

We had lunch the other day. He said, 'Boy it's great to be a writer. Isn't it?"

I'm working on my new book', he said.

'Which one is that?', I asked.

He laughed, 'I know what you're getting at. It's the fourth one I've started this year. But this one is different. I'm going to finish this one.'

'Good', I said. 'What's the title?'

'Haven't quite made up my mind yet. But I'm working on it — whenever I can spare the time. '

'For cripes sake, John. You'll never get it done that way. You're a good writer. Take the time.'

'That's what I'm planning on doing as soon as I complete my article on Trout Fishing In The Adirondacks.'

'Who are you writing it for, John?'

'Haven't decided, yet.'

'John, you know better than that. Every Mag requires a different slant. You damn well better know who you're writing for, or you end up just spinning your wheels.'

'Not always. I've sold a few without sending out queries — no research — nothing. I simply write 'em; stick them in the mail; and pray.'

'That is pure unadulterated luck. Why don't you study the market first? Find out who's looking for what. You could sell fifty times more stuff.'

'Yeah, but who wants to waste time counting words? Editors would be smarter if they'd print it no matter what length and cut out the silly ads.'

'John, that's like saying a merchant should turn out his store lights and sell you a shirt with the sleeves nine inches too long. Why not tailor your piece right in the first place?'

'You've asked me that before. I plan on doing it — when I can find more time. Right now my main concern is to finish my book and get it published.'

'How many pages have you done?'

'Hard to say. Maybe thirty or forty. My desk is loaded with stuff.'

'Why don't you clean off your desk and work on one manuscript at a time?'

'One of these days, I'm gonna do that. Just as soon as I get caught up.'

'What are you waiting for?'

'You mean about getting caught up? I sorta plan on doing it by next Monday; or no later than Thursday; unless something interferes. Then I may have to delay it a day or two. But that's about the limit.'

'Thanks. That tells me a lot. Let's get back to the book. When will you have it finished? What's your deadline?'

'No special deadline. It may look unfinished right now. But once I really get going, I'll have it finished in no time.'

'Yeah, I know. About 40,000 books get published every year — and maybe a million more will never get finished — just lay gathering dust in attics, files, or desks.'

'Not mine. I'm gonna finish this one first — then go back and finish the other three I been working on.'

'How?'

'No problem. I got it all figured out. I'll start typing at nine every morning, and keep typing 'til eleven. No more staring out the window wondering if the fish are biting; no more walks down to the lake to get in the mood.

'I'll take a couple of hours for lunch. Then get right back to typing from one until three in the afternoon. No more dips in the pool to keep my body in shape until after I get at least four pages done every day.'

'You mean no more dawdling of any kind? No more sitting there meditating while you file your nails; check your supply of paper clips, pencils, erasable paper, ribbons, file folders, felt tip pens, kleenex, index cards, cough drops.

'No more trips to the bathroom to see if you put your toothbrush away; no more computing the number of days until Christmas or determining when Easter comes next year.'

'That's right. No more stalling. You told me before that if I'm going to write, I gotta write. I've been deliberating about it a lot.

'This time I've made up my mind. I will stick to a daily schedule — unless, of course, mitigating factors rise and I am forced to defer for a day or so.'

'That's great, John', I said as we ended our lunch.

I know he will be pleased when I send him an entry blank for the SuperPRO Hall of Hestitation. He's becoming very sophisticated and deserves recognition.

GARDEN OF GOSH

If you are strictly a city dweller who has never lived in anything other than a high rise in a concrete jungle, you may not understand my neighbors and their love for gardening.

But that's okay. They don't understand each other either.

Maybe it's because they have such different ways of making things grow. One has potential for our club. The other will never make it — at least not in the gardening category. Even the untrained eye can detect the distinction in their styles.

Big Richard is a giant of a man, who crushed many an opposing lineman with his ferocious 275 pound tackles during his football career. But now he is as gentle as the Jolly Green Giant who tends his garden with loving care.

He is an organic gardener who uses no chemical fertilizers; nor pesticides. He simply cooperates with Mother

147

Nature to ward off killer bugs and ugly weeds by interplanting a variety of vegetables in the same raised bed.

This intermingling of companion plants is not haphazard. It is studied and carefully done. For instance, onion and garlic among the cabbage plants.

In addition to this, marigolds are sprinkled here and there among the plants. They add a touch of beauty to the beds. But their primary job is to discourage certain plant-eating flies and bugs from moving into the neighborhood.

I feel certain that the EEOC would not sanction such gross discrimination. They would probably rule in favor of our other gardening neighbor.

He permits anything and everything to habitat his garden. That is not Manuel's intention.

In mid-March, when the snows are melting off the mountain, he says, 'This year I am going to have the best garden in the county. No weeds. No bugs.'

Like Richard, he is full of enthusiasm and good intentions as he looks forward to the growing season. He knows he could have ordered his seeds a month or so ago from the seed catalogs and saved five or ten per cent.

However, since he put off doing so, he said, 'I'll buy from the local Garden Way store. Then I can see what I'm getting .'

That is partially true. He gets to select the Burpee Seed packages from a display case rather than from a seed catalog. Plus he does not have to compute the five percent discount for ordering early.

As an experienced procrastinator, he knows that this deprives him of the pleasure of planting tomato, cabbage, broccoli, pepper, cauliflower, and other plants in flats in his small greenhouse during the snowy winter months.

He says, 'What the heck. I can always buy plants from Garden Way. Let them run the risk of half of the plants dying from blight or other crap. I can buy bigger plants and have ripe tomatoes before Richard does.'

What's wrong with that?

Philosophically, nothing.

After all, why should a SuperPRO do something today that can be postponed until a later date and then accomplished with far less risk, effort, and time expenditure?

If you have aspirations for becoming a SuperPRO. I hope you have been carefully taking notes about these various techniques as they appear in this guidebook. I may not get around to summarizing them.

Much better you should remember them in proper context, anyway.

Which means we better stick with Manuel a while longer to see how he makes out with his garden.

He says, 'I might better spend time in my garden doing cleanup work that I had to delay last Fall. If the snow hadn't come so early, I still might have gotten it done.'

'You would be way, way ahead', says Big Richard. 'Turning that stuff under in the Fall helps make humus, lessens weed growth, and disease carryover.'

' I know. But you can't expect me to be in the garden during hunting and football season.' replies Manuel. 'You must get out of work a lot earlier than I do.'

'No. I come straight home. I skip Happy Hour with the guys.'

'Yeah. Well not me. I ain't about to miss out on what's happening at the office. I can always do my gardening on weekends.'

And he could — if he would. But each weekend that he planned to buy his seeds, he was deterred — by one thing or another. Not having the seeds, he postponed turning the soil. Which, of course, perpetuated delay when he did get the seeds.

However, he had greenery. Lots of it. Weeds were growing prolifically; everywhere. He said, 'No problem. I'll just plow them under. Same as a cover crop.'

Finally he did. He was amazed to see that most of Big Richard's crops were growing profusely — and Manuel said, 'He must be force feeding them with fertilizer. Guess I'll do the same. Use a lot of it.'

He did. The results were disastrous. Some things grew too fast and spindly. Others turned yellow from an overdose of chemicals. And where he overloaded with horse manure, a bumper crop of new and exotic weeds sprang into being. All of this was happening even before he found time to buy his tomato, broccoli, and other plants.

On June 10, he said to his wife, 'No more danger of frost. Guess I'll buy my tomato plants this weekend.'

'Don't know where you'll find them,'

she said. 'They were all sold out at Garden Way two weeks ago.'

' That's not very smart. Don't they realize that some people get unavoidably delayed and need to plant late? What's the matter with those people anyway?'

A setback like that can be very upsetting to a man's plans. Discourages him. So Manuel said, 'To Hell with it. Guess I'll start playing golf again this weekend.'

When it came to neglect, Manuel became increasingly proficient. As the summer wore on, he did less and less cultivating, little or no weeding, and seldom watered.

He extended his dilatoriness into the Fall months and failed to harvest what few crops had survived.

He said, 'Gosh! What went wrong? You'd think Mother Nature would let a guy run a little late on some things.'

Manuel is a shoo-in for SuperPRO.

HEALTH CARE

Many a city dweller is automatically eliminated from competition in the gardening group of procrastinators.

However, they have a field in which they traditionally excel. It's called the Health Care Field.

It's a dying shame that anyone wants to even reveal their procrastinatic skills in this field. And we would shun them were it not the duty of a research team to report things as they are — not as researchers would like them to be.

Cigarette smokers pick up the easiest points. Why? Probably because they maintain the greatest visiblilty. They can be seen day or night at every level of our social strata.

You have probably heard,
'Breathes there a man with soul so dead,
Who nea'r to himself has said,
I am going to stop smoking
Once and for all
Just as soon as I take
A couple more puffs
And my nerves quiet down.'

He contemplates; he plans; he makes resolutions; he talks with reformed ex-smokers; he reads how-to-break-the-habit books; he tries hypnosis, pills, gum, he listens to statistics; she fears breast cancer; he lung cancer.

She participates in the annual One Day Non-Smoke-athon; She stops puffing smoke toward other people; he butts out after a couple of drags — fifty times a day.

He even reads the Warning label on the pack.

What do we end up with? Someone who is going to stop smoking — tomorrow, next week, next month — or as soon as the pressure from a rush order at the office is completed.

'Then I will stop smoking. I know that taking care of my health is important,' says the SuperPRO. 'And I'm going to do something about mine — real soon. Yes I am.'

What do we end up with? Someone who is going to stop smoking — tomorrow, next week, next month — or as soon as the pressure from a rush order at the office is completed.

'Then I will stop smoking. I know that taking care of my health is important,' says the SuperPro. 'And I'm going to do something about mine — real soon. Yes. I am.'

The die-hard smoker has developed anti-non-smoking resistance comparable to the legendary survival ability of the cockroach.

Karen Karter is such a person. But now her motivation is being squelched. Last week her doctor said, 'Karen, stop smoking — or you'll be dead — in six months.'

And just yesterday, while shopping in an exclusive shop on the avenue, she found the most darling new head gear. It's called Smokers Bubble.

It's styled beautifully; comes in pink, blue, or burgundy. It fits over one's head like an outer-spacewalker's helmet. Each puff of smoke is retained within the helmet in a George Burns type filtration system. It is approved by the Environmental Protection Agency.

One problem. Remember when your kid brother yelled from the bathroom, 'Look, Ma, no hands.' Well this kind of smoking takes the same kind of concentration. Get the cigarette started, slip the Bubble over your head, and keep it going until finished.

Karen will consult her doctor to see if he approves of this euphoric method. She would like to postpone 'being dead in six months.'

If he's skeptical, at least she can continue to put off buying heavier winter clothing. Last winter when hospitalized with pneumonia, she was told, 'Karen, forget style. Wear clothing that will keep you warm and protect your health.'

Why should she be different than all the other working girls in the city?

KEEPING FIT

There are some exercise freaks who tend to distort the image of city dwellers. They go jogging or biking in the park; enroll in exercise classes; join health spas; play handball, tennis, or squash daily; swim twenty lengths of the 'Y' pool; pump iron; or do almost anything to introduce bodily stress.

Isn't there enough stress in the workplace?

A dedicated procrastinator knows how to avoid that stuff until later in life. Time enough to rebuild the body after it's had a chance to run down.

If you ever get around to it, physical check-ups will tell you.

Health Care and Keeping Fit are such broad and all encompassing subjects that it is impossible to deal with them extensively because of editor space restrictions.

Suffice it to say that SuperPROS devote their efforts to at least the following:

Put off dental check-ups until you are in agony — preferably Saturday midnight on a holiday week end.

Postpone eye exams — once you have your driver's license.

Ignore high fever — only means you're hot.

Delay getting braces for the kid's teeth — she never smiles anyway.

Defer surgery — get 2nd, 3rd,4th, and 5th opinions.

Someone may say you don't need it.

Why buy health or hospital insurance? You're healthy as a horse.

Refrain from fiddling with your breasts. A little swelling might look good.

Delay going to the hospital until your appendix bursts. What are emergency rooms for, anyway?

Waffle about seeing the doctor — maybe you are only a little late this month.

Put off cutting your toenails — lots of people get sore feet.

Defer vacations — how can a doctor tell you're headed for a nervous breakdown?

RATIONAL EMOTIVE PSYCHOTHERAPY

In a book of this nature, it is only fair to let you know that my researchers discovered a counter culture which is, without a doubt, adamantly and diametrically opposed to the practice of procrastination.

In fact, some of its proponents make lots of money trying to cure us of the habit of procrastinating. Many are highly educated, with years of experience in the application of psychiatric medicine.

In no way would we attempt to cast reflections on those who are dedicated professionals. The world needs doctors who are capable of diagnosing, treating, and trying to prevent mental disorders.

Their service to mankind is immeasurable. We need them.

What we do not need is charlatans — the ones who refuse to recognize that marching to a different drummer keeps us from becoming mindless robots.

They are the ones who go around endlessly preaching, 'Don't put things off. Do it today.'

It is hard to quarrel with the underlying wisdom of that thought. But if a person does not adhere strictly to that admonition, it does not mean that they have an emotional problem.

So why create one for them?

Why generate a self-imposed guilt complex on an individual for postponing something scheduled for today?

Was Rome built in a day?

Or an even bigger project by the master architect — Did the Lord create the universe in a single day?

Heavens no!

Our stairway to perfection is not easy to climb. We can't even see where it ends. That is as it should be. Mystery adds zest and intrigue to our lives.

When some of us postpone an action, it becomes a mystery as to when — if ever, we will get it accomplished.

If you are the kind of person who cannot tolerate that kind of existence, — one who becomes totally frustrated with anything which you must postpone — then you may need something like REP.

When I first heard of REP, I tried to look it up. Would you believe that we could find only two Books-In-Print on the subject of procrastination? And it took nearly six weeks to get them.

However, they were worth waiting for. They shed light on what is being done in the area of cognitive behavior therapy as relates to overcoming procrastination.

In order for you to also have a better understanding, allow me to quote from the psychologist — psychotherapist co-authors who said, 'Cognitive behavior therapy is a psychotherapeautic methodology that represents a synthesis of action-oriented systems, such as behavior therapy, behavior modification, and rational emotive pshychotherapy.'

Considerable emphasis was placed on rational emotive psychotherapy (REP). You should read these books if you want to broaden your knowledge about the subject.

I think I have already told you that THERE SEEMS TO BE NO UNIVERSALLY EFFECTIVE METHOD to overcome procrastination.

Probably so.

But is that necessarily bad? I don't think so.

Some people regard sex as being bad.

Some of it is. But would you advocate eliminating all of it, because some is bad?

No way!

Why make ourselves feel inadequate, hostile, or emotionally disturbed because we participate in this universal phenomenon of procrastination?

Let's learn to live with it.

Perhaps one way to do that is to continue to search out role models.

For instance, you may pick up some good pointers from Rosemary Proctor. She is very good at what her six brothers have taught her to do — and what she likes to do best — auto mechanics.

But does she venture forth to find a job doing it? NO! She hesitates; she waits; she postpones. She doesn't even file an application for a mechanic's job.

'What are you afraid of?' asks her big brother, Randy.

'I don't look like a grease-pit monkey. They'll laugh at me.'

'Baby, you're the most beautiful doll who ever screwed a set of clamps on a radiator. We laugh at you all the time.'

'That's different. You're my brothers.'

'Forget the sexist viewpoint, baby. That's old hat. Today you can do anything you want to do.'

'Yeah, maybe on paper. But just wait until I try to get that kind of job. They'll laugh — a woman mechanic?'

'Hey, baby. If they laugh at you, we'll cut off their balls.'

Under the circumstances, this seems like an appropriate course of action. But it cannot be officially condoned.

Furthermore, if they remove the road-block, Rosemary would lose her prime excuse for not taking action — might even apply and land the job. Do you want her to be faced with the dilemma of finding something new to be fearful about in order to build points toward SuperPRO?

You know as well as I that there are traditional male or female job categories. Despite the new laws, many people do not feel comfortable about breaking established patterns that have existed for years and years. These provide an excellent base for inertia.

What would happen if one of those six brothers wanted to assume a non-traditional role? Let's say a phone operator; a hairdresser; a house husband; a chambermaid; or a strip-tease artist. Would the brothers again wield a knife?

Now that the barriers have been broken, we have lost access to many, many potential SuperPROS — whose inhibitions and fear of being laughed at are no longer valid.

Our membership may suffer because of this, but that's the risk we run in a club that maintains such rigid standards.

 DOUBLE EXPOSURE

SOCIAL GRACE

Certain people in our society have a keen perception of what is appropriate and right in maintaining friendly relations with relatives and others in our society. Some are so good at it that they are called aristocrats.

My Aunt Caroline aspires to be such a person.

She throws formal, elegant, and frequent parties. She also sends cards — hundreds of cards. She is very meticulous in selecting the right card for every occasion. She sends only the best.

The month of June is traditionally a hectic month for her. For instance, in June:

We received a gorgeous Happy Anniversary card — we were married in December.

June got her annual Happy Birthday card. June was born in January.

Scotty was elated with his Graduation card and the enclosed check — even though he graduated on May 5.

My wife appreciated the Get Well Soon card. We paid the hospital bill five months ago.

Smitty tore up his Congratulations On Your Promotion card. He's been fired.

Eleanor, whose first husband died last November received a Sympathy card that said, 'To Comfort You In Your Sorrow'. It was waiting for her when she and her new husband returned from their Bermuda honeymoon.

No one questions Aunt Caroline's good intentions. She wants to remember important events in peoples' lives and make them feel happy.

Her cards do that.

Never has a card arrived on time.

But I assure you they are remembered.

MIGHT NEED IT SOMEDAY

Uncle Len deprives the town landfill (city dump) of an enormous amount of what some people classify as junk.

He is not a dump picker. I doubt that he has ever been to a dumpsite. He is a purist. Every item he obtains is carefully pre-screened in its natural environment.

He has no formal education in the art of postponing the demise of useful items. His is a natural talent — first detected when as a kid he was heard to say, 'Don't throw that away. I might be able to use it someday.'

Even without parental guidance or encouragement, his uncommon aptitude developed to the point where he is now recognized as a connoisseur.

Last week, a Sears Serviceman replace two slightly rusty bolts and nuts on Uncle Len's freezer. Uncle said, 'Don't throw those away. I might be able to use them someday.'

'I planned the same, ' said the Serviceman.

'Okay. Toss you for 'em.'

Kindred souls in this field are willing to gamble. The Sears guy called 'tails', and Uncle Len lost.

He smiled and tucked his two-headed coin back in his pocket.

Most of the time, he wins.

That is unimportant.

What counts is that his crusade for saving items from destruction prevails.

His basement, garage, attic, and den are crammed with items he 'might be able to use someday.'

One problem. How to find the item he needs. Each year he says, 'I gotta find time to organize this stuff.'

In the meantime, he is happy to hear a major winery paraphrase his motto, 'Nothing of mine will go before its time.'

PHOTO ALBUM

Where is your photo album? You know the one with the kids growing up.

What are all those pictures stuffed in envelopes halfway thru the album? Why all the blank pages? You've got tons of photos to choose from.

Weren't you the one who said, 'We are not going to be like your parents. We will have a picture of every important event in our kids' lives — neatly arranged so everybody can re-live their growing up.'

You certainly had good intentions. Not everyone buys such a large expensive album.

Let's take a look at it.

'That must be Susie. Or was it Johnny who had that ball when he was a year old? I think it must be Susie. Johnny never had that much hair when he was little. But little girls aren't supposed to sit like that, so it just might be Johnny.

'How come we didn't get around to writing in the name?'

'Now this is Susie. Remember how proud she was to win that spelling bee?'

'When was this shot taken? I don't remember ever seeing it before. How come Susie wasn't in the picture? Oh, she took the picture.'

'Now there she is. But where are all the pictures of her growing up? How can we call this an album? Let's start getting this thing organized — sometime this week or next when we have more time. No sense in putting it off any longer.'

You know, and I know that they are just trying to build up SuperPRO points. They have found the photo album bit to be one of the most fertile breeding grounds around.

Everyone has good intentions — but over the years the photo album continues to offer great opportunities for deferred action; unpasted prints; people, places, and dates not identified; prints left forgotten at some drug store; film undeveloped and remaining in camera the last two years.

My, oh my.

Be sure you have a photo album available. Two or three would be even better.

And be sure to include a picture of the family homestead so everyone can reminisce about their humble beginnings.

YOU OR I COULD HAVE

Nelson Goodson is unhappy with us. He is also unhappy with himself. He insists that he should be recognized as a full fledge SuperPRO. Our Board decrees that he should have only associate member status.

The Board is right. Nelson belongs to the 'I Could Have' crowd, which is really a splinter group. They live in the past; talk of the past; and dream of what they could have done.

In pleading his case, Nelson said, 'I could have become a millionaire last year. I saw Coleco stock selling at 12. It took off and went to 65 within months. I could have borrowed from the bank; bought 20,000 shares at 11 or 12; sold at 65; and made a bundle.'

'Why didn't you?' I asked.

'Well, — I could have,' he replied.

A similar outlook is shown by Simon Seamen. We were at the race track the other day when number eight and five paid $1,312 in the daily double. I tore up my two dollar ticket on seven and four.

Simon said, 'Damn. Look what I could have won. I could have had twenty bucks on that. Look. See. I had it marked right here on my program.'

No question about it. He had it marked. He also tore up five tickets on other combos that 'could have' won according to Simon's thinking.

Why does Simon act like that? Going broke on 'could haves' must be frustrating.

The same kind of thinking prevails with Wayne Howard. He looks at the Shopping Mall and says, 'I could have bought all that land at ten dollars an acre. I could have made a mint instead of being stuck with my house on the edge of a traffic turnstile. I could have sold the house too, before the mall was built.'

Wayne has a legitimate gripe. He could have.

Wayne's brother, William, is an amateur inventor — with patents pending. When he saw Rubic's Cube come on the market a few years ago, he said, 'I could have invented that.'

And a few months later, Bill's wife read a book — 'Solutions to Rubic's Cube' — number one on the best seller lists. She cried, 'I could have written that.'

As an alert student of the gentle art of procrastination, you should carefully note the line of differentiation.

Do you find any prophets among the 'I Could Have' crowd?

No. They are historians. They revel in the past.

Genuine Procrastinators don't do that. They don't bemoan lost opportunities. They are planners. They look to the future. Whatever it may be, SuperPROS WILL DO IT — as soon as they get around to it.

Which would you rather be?

CLASSIC COLLECTIONS

Mike is a collector of a far different sort. He specializes. He has two distinct collections. Trains and toys. Both are said to be very valuable.

And I'll bet they are.

He is very knowledgeable and has been very discriminating in his accumulation of rare specimens. He attends train conventions all over the USA. He reads collectors magazines and carefully researches the history of every model. Mike knows values. He is a very shrewd trader.

He is also a cabinet maker and builder.

He constructed his own home, which includes a gigantic room in the basement for proper display and running of model trains. He also built two glass display cases in which to place some models on exhibit.

But what has he done about his valuable collections? Nothing really — except to continue to be a compulsive collector of trains and toys.

Cardboard boxes occupy every inch of available space in Mike's seven room house and basement. That includes under the beds; in the half-bath; in the hallway; on the basement stairs; on top of the fridge; and sometimes on the dining room table.

To the untrained eye, it would appear as if they were getting ready to move to another house. However, his wife loves the $160,000 place despite its 'storage house' inconveniences. Dusting is difficult.

I asked Mike, 'What are you going to do with your collection?'

'I'm going to establish my own Classic Trains and Toys Museum, and publish a newsletter for dealers and train buffs — sometime in the near future. May even retire from my job early; or give up fishing.'

PROCRASTINATOR'S PRAYER

BY
Richard J. Sandora

Lord, grant me the strength to undertake
All the daily chores I seem to forsake.
Strip my hands from within my pockets,
Make my ambition flare like rockets;
But please leave me time to contemplate.

Oh, Heavenly Father, help me in my fight
To overcome my passion for burning daylight.
Fill my heart with fervor, zeal and drive.
Help my dormant vitality to come alive;
But let me still have pause to watch the
      hummingbird's flight.

I pray, let me think 'Today', not 'Tomorrow'
Relieve my guilt, relieve my sorrow,
For not having yet complete
What I said I would last week;
But let me continue to greet the sparrow.

Lord, let my ardor for attainment be fervent.
Please allow me to make a covenant
That I will no longer delay
What needs to be done this day;
Just as soon as I care for this plant.

Lord, I know that the Hobgoblin of Procrastination
Will cause me no worry, tears or fears,
For I've been made in the image
Of someone putting things off for
Nigh on two thousand years.

DON'T CRY

Carol Lauer, one of my most dedicated researchers, went way beyond the call of duty in tracking and recording the lifetime activities of a dropout SuperPRO.

She followed him right to the very edge of the Pearly Gates.

It would take too long to share all of her findings with you. However, there's time for some of the highlights from Bob Martin's misguided career.

Through the magic of hindsight, Carol reached back into Bob's past - way back.

In Carol's first taped recording, we hear Bob's father say, 'You gotta do what your Mother tells you. Don't put off doing your homework one minute longer. Go to your room, right now! And don't dilly-dally. Don't make any excuses. Do it.'

'But, Dad.'

'No stalling. Go!'

In Carol's next tape, we hear Bob's boss say, 'There is absolutely no reason for delay. You must do your reports on time, or you will be fired.'

'But, I can explain.'

'Don't make excuses. Just do your work on time. What do you think I'm paying you for?'

Next we hear Bob's wife say, 'Robert, you should do my mother's income tax first. Then you should do all the things around here that need doing before you even think about playing golf. Why do you always put off doing what you should do? If you don't start doing what you should do when you should do it, I'm leaving you.'

' My goodness, Carol,' I said. 'Is that all this guy hears — must do; gotta do; no excuses; no delays; should do; and threats from everyone?'

'That's right,' she replied.

'How can he take all this?'

'He couldn't take so much pressure. He got to feeling that procrastination is a horrible, unforgiveable thing. No authority figure would tolerate any part of it. He developed feelings of guilt, rejection, and low self-esteem.'

'That's a shame. There's no need to feel that way. He should have faith in himself. Everybody procrastinates.'

'I told him procrastinating, at least a little, is a good safety valve. But he was afraid to risk it.'

Then Carol played her final tape. Bob is at the Pearly Gates and we hear him say , 'St. Peter, here's my record. As you can see I did

every thing as I was told. There are no blemishes on my record.'

'I won't need your records, ' said St. Peter. 'You can enter. Walk right in.'

While Bob is entering, he says, 'I thought heaven was a happy place. Why are those people in the corner crying?'

'They just now found out I don't keep records.'

THE MAÑANA ATTITUDE

Perhaps our culture — trying to jam too many things into too little time — is mainly responsible for the pandemic growth of what is known as the Mañana Attitude — 'why do today what you can put off until tomorrow.'

How easy it is to fool yourself into believing 'I don't really have time to do this today, but it will be very easy to do this tomorrow.'

Under the pressure of too little time, that rationalization becomes valid and soon begets good reasons for postponing all kinds of important things. Before you know it, the lies you tell youself become truths to justify your dilatory habits.

The reason I am pointing this out is to help you keep current on what is happening in the field. If a cultural revolution is occurring, it is far better to be on the cutting edge of such a movement.

Would you want to be the last to learn that a mañana attitude can provide enormous fringe benefits?

For instance, in the helter skelter world of trying to squeeze too many things into too little time, mañana often acts as a shield to help preserve sanity.

Very few of your friends and associates will object to your maintaining some degree of sanity, providing you don't start driving them crazy.

174

And the best way to drive them bananas is to promise to do something, then don't do it on time. Promise to do something else. And again, resort to mañana.

They will soon forget the underlying reason for your protective shield. All they will remember is that part of our culture which says, 'Be ambitious. Be aggressive. Be involved in everything. Push, push, push. Never hesitate.'

With friends like that, you won't need enemies.

What you need is more sophistication. No need to retreat into your closet. Neither should you flaunt your mañana attitude. Know what to do when you get caught.

Take a lesson from Mayor Petersen.

When publicly confronted with charges that he had failed to turn over certain sums of money to the City Treasurer, he said, 'No problem. Merely an administrative oversight. I will deliver all the money to the treasurer — sometime tomorrow.'

You may have wondered, when you first saw the cover of this book, why anyone would herald it as an 'almost' complete guide rather than a complete guide to NOT getting things done, — on time.

But I ask you, 'how can anyone write a truly complete guide to such a complicated subject?'

Is it not better to establish creditability at the outset so that readers will understand that there is more to the subject?

In fact, my researchers are still compiling data, both from the archives of my ancestors and from current practices among procrastinators.

In addition to that, I think it is important to encourage readers to expand their horizons and develop some techniques of their own. Even so, I will try to squeeze in a few more prototypes, and random observations, so as to keep your mind in gear.

You will find it is easy to spot the most talented procrastinators. They are the ones who always say, 'I work best under pressure.'

Of these, one of the greatest procrastinators I have ever known was a Japanese Kamikassee pilot— on his 50th mission.

It seems that all through life we are forever being told, 'DON'T PROCRASTINATE,' Yet, one of the giants in the world of business, General Foods Corporation, runs a very eye-catching advertisement in national magazines with four important headline words — HOW TO PROCRASTINATE TASTEFULLY. What a marvelous way to recognize the facts of life and encourage people to procrastinate and enjoy it with a feeling of relaxation and propriety.

This may translate to some of us as, 'Goofing off in style.' What's wrong with that? Who wants to be a slob about it?

By now, you should have developed all sorts of pleasant routines to distract yourself. But don't dawdle for extended periods of time over undone work, worrying over where to begin.

EITHER DECIDE TO DO IT or DON'T DO IT AT ALL, but don't feel bad or guilty about it. Why work yourself into a frenzy? To err is human. To procrastinate is also human.

With practice, you can become very adept at doing things late. One way is to create an image of being overburdened with more important problems; with pressing matters which must take priority.

While maintaining this image, you can lie to yourself and say,'As soon as I get to it, I will spontaneously knock-off all the work that has piled up during my orgy of procrastination.'

You can also claim, 'I'm too tired. I've got no energy.' Focus on how dreadful it feels to get up and get going. If you really concentrate on how tired you feel, you can soon become totally exhausted, without doing a damn thing. What amazing things our minds can do for us.

Another classic ploy is to say, 'As soon as my financial difficulties get straightened out, I'll catch up.' If you haven't thought of this one by now, you may lack the initiative to become a SuperPRO. Be aware that no matter how many guidebooks you may read on the subject, you must also do some thinking of your own.

I would be remiss if I did not point out that the secret desire of many a dedicated procrastinator is the still small voice from within, which often says, 'It may go away — by doing nothing.'

One of the great rewards for being a SuperPRO is that you never need to feel bored. You will do your best to maintain a series of incompleted tasks — and thus always have something to look forward to.

Don't let the admonition on the next page disenchant you. It is intended for less hardy souls who have decided to reform.

Perhaps this is the place to remind you that I eagerly await hearing from you (whenever you get around to it) with documentation of the exploits of your favorite SuperPRO. If you have ideas and worthy suggestions for etching the name of each great SuperPRO upon the Soul of Destiny. Please also send those along. NO HURRY.

A

TUIT

How many times have you said:
"I'LL DO IT AS SOON AS I GET
AROUND TO IT"
NO MORE EXCUSES
NOW YOU CAN EASILY DO IT
FOR NOW AT LAST, YOU'VE GOT

A ROUND TUIT

A GENTLE REMINDER

Did you ever say to yourself, 'SOMEDAY, I'm going to write my own book.'?

Now that you understand the real power of procrastination, you can continue to put it off, and put it off; until someday you can proudly proclaim, 'I Could Have.'

OR

You can get some meaningful guidance from any of our following titles:

How To Make Money Writing
And Selling Simple Information $15.00
Why Specialize in "How-To" Books 3.00
Why Write A Full Size Book 3.00
Which Books Sell Best 3.00

If your favorite bookseller does not have a copy of any of the above, you may order direct from the publisher, by sending check or money order for total amount. (We pay postage.) For a complete list of titles, please send stamped, self-addressed envelope to:

BARNES - BOOKS
FORT ANN, N.Y. 12827

KEY PHRASES

for
SOPHISTICATED SuperPROS

If you are to live up to your potential as a SuperPRO, you will need to develop beyond the one word reply (as is used in Vermont).

Weave some of the following phrases into your conversation so that others may recognize your degree of sophistication and proficiency as a SuperPRO;

as soon as I get around to it
after I finish this
take it under advisement
whenever it's feasible
waiting for more favorable conditions

when I feel in the mood
a little later
when the time is right
not right now
wait until I'm fully prepared

have been meaning to
cannot seem to find time to
maybe tomorrow
let's postpone action
real soon

not just yet
going to put off
send it to the committee

as soon as I can get to it
real soon

sometime later on
let's table it for now
this needs more study
put it off until
next week would be better

what difference will a day make
why do it today
tomorrow will be just as good
there will be lots of tomorrows

To those of you who have refined the technique,
SuperPROS everywhere will say, 'Many Happy Delays'.

THERE'S MORE TO TELL

(as soon as I get around to it.)

SuperPRO-crastinators I KNOW.

MY TOP TEN FAVORITES
for the
HALL OF HESITATION

1.

2.

3.

4.

5.

6.

7.

8.

9.

10.

ASPIRING SuperPROs I KNOW

I COULD HAVE

List of things I could have done, but kept putting off
— and putting off — until the opportunity was gone.

1.

2.

3.

4.

5.

6.

7.

8.

9.

10.

11.

12.

13.

THINGS I CAN PUT OFF
UNTIL TOMORROW

HERE'S WHAT YOU PROCRASTINATE ABOUT

(Make list and give this book to your favorite procrastinator. Check appropriate selection.)

Spouse_____

Best friend_____

Lover_____

Dad_____

Mom_____

Son_____

Daughter_____

Relative_____

Partner_____

Classmate_____

Roomy_____

Past due account_____

Good friend_____

Other_____

Here's the list of things YOU keep putting off — and putting off — and may never even get done:

1.

2.

3.

4.

5.

6.

7.

8.

9.

10.

(see next page)

Yes, there's lots more:

11.

12.

13.

14.

15.

16.

17.

18.

19.

20.

WHY I AM DEDICATED
to
THE GENTLE ART
of
PROCRASTINATION

(write your own reasons)

THINGS I PROCRASTINATE ABOUT

Write a statement — or put it in list form — whichever will best portray your ability for NOT getting things done — on time.

BUZZ WORDS FOR PROCRASTINATORS

If you are to become a SuperPRO, you must learn to recognize key words that will identify you as a member of the 'inner circle'.

Here they are:

later
soon
someday
awhile
after
postpone
delay
defer
withhold
plan
time
sometime
expect
intend
future
dilatory
planning
contemplate
waffle
tardy
dilatoriness
maybe
mañana

Of course there are other words you can use. Some of them should not be printed here. The important thing is that you gradually introduce these words into your vocabulary — whenever you get around to it.

ABOUT THE AUTHOR

Tradition dictates that biographical materials be written in the third person. To me that would be inconsistent with my style of writing. Why be coy? Much better that I continue to communicate on a one - to - one basis.

Despite my endless fascination with the art of procrastination, I have found time to write for dailies, weeklies, pulps, slicks, trade journals, house organs, and my own nationally syndicated column, 'Our People — USA'.

My writings also include manuals, booklets, folios, and books — one of which is enjoying sales in 46 nations.

I could have written more — except I was too busy making a living, devoting time to my family, immersing myself in community affairs, tending my garden, and helping others.

Writing fills a compulsive, obsessive need within me. Already I am planning on writing another book — as soon as 'I get around tuit'.

HERE'S WHAT OTHERS SAY:

"SuperPRO is a super funny book. In fact, it is a storehouse of laughs."
> —Dr. William L. Bitner, III, President of the Independent Bankers Association of New York State

"SuperPRO-crastinators establishes Joe Barnes as a writer to be reckoned with."
> —Arthur S. Fisher, former editor(retired) of The Glens Falls Times.

"A-OKAY. Very well done. I enjoyed it immensely."
> —Basil S. Dwyer, retired educator.

"This is a most enjoyable book — very appealing because it is very humorous and one we can all relate to."
> —Sandy Adams, Radio WWSC Talk Show Hostess.

"This is a marvelous book — destined to be a best seller in the coming year."
> —Al Gallasso, editor Book Dealers World.

"Controversial humor at its best: amusing, witty and highly recommendable."
> —Neil Michaels, editor Book Business Mart.